How to
THRIVE
UNDER THE NDIS

A Pathway to Sustainability
for Service Providers

How to
THRIVE
UNDER THE NDIS

A Pathway to Sustainability
for Service Providers

FRAN CONNELLEY

'Fran Connelley's book is a must read "thrival guide" for Board members, CEOs, executives and managers of disability organisations in Australia right now – at this time of huge and exciting (but for some, daunting) change. It puts the case persuasively for why it is not only possible to be both "market driven" and "mission driven", but that it is the person-centred, absolutely correct, AND essential thing to do. And it provides a highly practical, step-by-step guide for how to do it. There is an emphasis on small and medium organisations; not just because some of the challenges are different, but also because Ms Connelley's (and my) view is that people with disabilities will be better served if there is a choice and diversity of excellent "niche" local and specialist providers alongside the larger more mainstream ones.'

Roger West, Director & Principal Consultant, WestWood Spice

'I think the biggest challenge for the sector relates to innovation. I think we carry a responsibility in the coming years to get in and build new, completely different service models; not repackaged old models, but real innovation which truly meets customer needs.'

Laura O'Reilly, CEO Fighting Chance

'People will simply walk away if you can't individually design and deliver services that meet their needs. They don't want the institutional "whole of life" support model. You must be prepared to innovate, be prepared to partner and be prepared to put people with a disability first.'

Lorna Sullivan, Director of Disability Services, Uniting Care Queensland

Dedicated to Frank, Meg, Sophie and Paul with love and thanks.

Author's note

It's a risky business writing a book about the National Disability Insurance Scheme. This Scheme has become the catalyst for a total reinvention of the Australian disability market and, as such, new details seem to be emerging daily regarding its implementation.

Understanding your customers and then understanding how to reinvent your organisation so it is actually customer-focused and market-driven is essential for your organisation's future.

As I write these words, the National Disability Services *State of the Disability Sector Report 2015* has just been released. This excellent document paints the picture of a sector searching for answers to legitimate questions and lacking resources or 'a clear map of the terrain ahead'.

The recent Joint Standing Committee's second progress report on the NDIS noted that, with only ten months until the implementation of the transition phase of the Scheme on 1 July 2016, only two states – NSW and Victoria – had signed bilateral agreements with the Commonwealth.

The report goes on to say, 'This by far is the most pressing issue the committee has repeatedly heard from all areas of the sector'.[1,2]

In the face of so much change and uncertainty, things can quickly become out of date. As a result, I have tried to focus on the fundamental market dynamics and the impacts of this massive social reform rather than the comings and goings of policy.

I should also say upfront that this book does not cover the operational challenges brought by the NDIS. Issues such as back office systems, rostering and I.T. fall outside my skillset. (I also feel there are solutions on the market that address these issues.)

What it does cover are the critical strategic issues that must be resolved to ensure that, at the end of your organisational

---

1   Progress report on the implementation and administration of the National Disability Insurance Scheme, 12 November 2015 © Commonwealth of Australia 2015.

2   Bilaterial agreements have since been signed for Tasmania, South Australia and some sites in northern Queensland.

transformation, you have customers who are happy to pay for the services you deliver because they meet their needs and life goals better than anything else available. Without the customer, everything else is meaningless.

Over the last eight years I've been privileged to work with some wonderful disability organisations and meet some extraordinary staff, parents, aunties, sisters, brothers, sons and daughters. I believe we need innovative, sustainable non-profit organisations of all sizes and shapes in order to truly provide choice and control to people with disabilities. Fewer providers will only bring less choice and less real innovation.

My sincere hope is that this book helps all providers delivering high-quality supports to achieve financial sustainability under the NDIS.

About the author

Fran Connelley is a strategic marketing specialist with over 20 years' experience in the non-profit sector, including eight years working with clients in the disability sector. She is passionate about broadening the funding base of wonderful charities.

She began her career in the Australian toy industry as a buyer with Toyworld and Group Product Manager with Hasbro Toys, where she managed brands such as Cabbage Patch Kids, Transformers and GI Joe. In this highly volatile market she learnt the value of great branding and storytelling to unlock new markets and revenue streams.

Fran has run her own consultancy, FC Marketing, for 21 years. She has worked with many non-profit clients, including Landcare Australia, Coastcare, Scalabrini Village, Sylvanvale Foundation, Allevia, Can Assist, The Young Endeavour Youth Scheme, the Australian National Botanic Gardens, The Royal Hospital for Women Foundation, TAD Disability Services and many others.

Fran is the author of the eGuide *Managing your Non Profit's Annual Report* and recently developed the *How to Thrive under the NDIS 7 Step Program*, a practical series of workshops for disability providers launching in April 2016.

Fran is an engaging speaker and facilitator and enjoys presenting group workshops on non-profit branding and strategic marketing.

For more information visit www.fcmarketing.com.au or email fran@fcmarketing.com.au.

First published in 2016 by FC Marketing
www.fcmarketing.com.au

National Library of Australia Cataloguing-in-Publication entry:

Creator: Connelley, Fran, author.
Title: How to thrive under the NDIS: a pathway to sustainability for service providers
ISBN: 9780994372604 (paperback)
Subjects: National Disability Insurance Scheme (Australia)
          Communication in services for people with disabilities – Australia.
          Disability insurance – Australia.
          People with disabilities – Services for – Australia.
          People with disabilities – Government policy – Australia.
          Long-term care insurance – Law and legislation – Australia.
Dewey Number: 362.40994

Book design and production by Michael Hanrahan Publishing
Cover design by Peter Reardon

10 9 8 7 6 5 4 3 2 1

Disclaimer

Contents

10 *Step* 7: Create your Action Plan   191

11 Where do we go now?   203

Introduction

The man in the wheelchair

I must have been about eight years old. I remember walking with my mum down a very crowded arcade in Chatswood and seeing an elderly gentlemen in a wheelchair wearing heavy woollen clothing and selling pens in the busiest, hottest corner on Victoria Avenue.

He looked like he'd been there all day. People were walking around him and past him. He was being totally ignored … and then my mum spotted him. Without hesitation, she went right up to him and bought two pens, shook his hand, smiled warmly, and chatted as if they were old friends. I'll never forget the look on his face. He struggled to speak, but he beamed back at her from ear to ear.

It was one of those moments that just sticks in your brain – freeze framed. Most of all, I remember how uncomfortable I felt. I was the cringing kid wishing my mum had never seen this guy, and yet all I saw was warmth shining out from both of them.

Cabbage Patch Kids

Fast forward 20 years and I'm Product Group Manager for Hasbro Toys, responsible for marketing all promotional toys. I was managing brands such as Transformers, GI Joe, My Little Pony, and then I landed the big one: Cabbage Patch Kids. Suddenly everything else was cleared from my plate.

Our sales team had done a brilliant job of selling the Cabbage Patch Kids toys into the market, and retailers everywhere were screaming for stock. I was responsible for shipping it. The tricky part was that each one of those Kids was unique. We're talking eye colour, skin colour, hair colour, body shape – you name it. I was facing container loads of body parts arriving in Sydney from China. Every one of those dolls had to be assembled based on a strict matrix which could not be altered, and it was my responsibility to find somewhere to assemble them.

It was then that I first heard the term 'sheltered workshops'. I remember visiting a number of these 'businesses' that provided employment to people with disabilities – and it was a shock. Many were dingy places, poorly run with bad lighting, except for one I found in Parramatta. (The disability sector has come a long way since then.)

Terry's workshop was a complete stand-out because he knew how to run a successful small business. The place was well organised, and super clean with lots of good natural lighting. Terry was an engaging guy with great people skills. He clearly loved his work and took great pride in his team. Not surprisingly, he landed the contract to assemble Cabbage Patch Kids and never let us down.

The introduction of the NDIS

Over the years I've raised funds to save coastlines, protect forests and provide equipment to detect cancer cells in an unborn child. However, it's the disability sector that keeps drawing me back.

Decades of government funding have created an inefficient market with heavy administration costs and lengthy delays on essential equipment and services. In 2008 Australia became one of the first countries to ratify the UN Convention on the rights of people with disabilities. And yet in terms of quality of life, Australia sits last in OECD rankings on poverty for people with disabilities.[3]

---

3   PwC, 'Disability expectations – Investing in a better life, a stronger Australia', Canberra, 2011.

The National Disability Insurance Scheme (NDIS) is about to fundamentally disrupt this market as it redirects funding away from organisations to people with disabilities. For the first time the consumer will become the paying customer, creating an entirely new marketplace.

Many disability organisations founded by well-meaning parents long ago will struggle to survive if they are unable to transform their organisation into a customer-service focused business.

So how do providers navigate the massive internal and external challenges ahead and achieve financial sustainability? This one question raises so many more: How do you transform from a mission-driven, community-based charity into a customer-centric small business? How is this all compatible with your mission? Is customer satisfaction different to what this sector calls being 'person-centred'? How do you maintain high-quality supports given the pricing constraints?

What's ahead

I've been fortunate to work with many non-profits over the last 20 years, and wanted to write a book to share my experiences and uncover the framework behind my best success stories. So, after much thought (and many extremely early mornings), this book outlines a straightforward brand-driven methodology customised to the needs of disability providers.

It also includes several interviews I've conducted with CEOs and sector thought leaders over the last few months. I am indebted to each of them for sharing so generously and providing me with invaluable case studies to support my methodology.

The first chapter covers an overview of the Australian disability sector. The second chapter then begins with demystifying marketing. I reframe the traditional definition of marketing to enable organisational 'buy-in' and to demonstrate that being commercial and being 'mission-driven' doesn't have to be a trade-off.

We then dive right into the 7 Steps:

Step 1) Know your market: Forget what you think you know and go out and do the research. Great marketing begins with your customer. You need data. This is not about you, your staff or your organisation. You need to look outside. Be aware of the emerging trends inside your own client base, in your local demographics, inside your industry, outside your industry and internationally. Watch, read, ask, listen, measure and evaluate.

Step 2) Revisit the fundamentals: We discuss the Vision and the Mission of the organisation. We then cover the critical need for market relevance, team 'buy-in' and visionary leadership to drive strategic growth.

Step 3) Build your brand: We discuss the role of the non-profit brand, the brand components, the style guide, the brand architecture, and unravel the link between the values that underpin your brand and building a high-performance culture. We then outline your brand stories and how to spread the word.

Step 4) Define your strategy: We discuss how to develop a winning strategy based on identifying your ideal market niche. We define strategic marketing and look at why strategic planning is tougher in the non-profit sector than anywhere else.

Step 5) Develop your strategic partnerships: We then look at a broad range of partnerships and the Living Community Model. Using this model you can build an ecosystem of future customers, donors, partners, sponsors, volunteers, grant-makers, community groups and supporters around your cause.

Steps 6) Customise your systems: Every existing system needs to be reviewed with your customer as its focus. We discuss non-profit parameters to measure your efficiency and effectiveness and introduce the end-to-end customer journey and some ideas for systematising the customer experience.

Step 7) Create your Action Plan: Strategy is nothing without action. This is about actions with outcomes not simply outputs. In this final chapter we look at how to develop your own strategic Marketing Action Plan and look at some other practical tools to assist in planning and monitoring your performance outcomes.

How to get the most out of this book

This book is for leaders in the disability sector who know they lack the branding and marketing expertise they need to thrive in the new choice-based landscape of the NDIS. After you've read it through you can easily dip into it as needed to find the right information at the right time.

I hope it helps your organisation capitalise on the market opportunities available right now and find the funds you need to make a long-term impact in the communities you serve.

Best of luck with your transition to the NDIS,

Fran Connelley
Sydney
January 2016

Chapter 1

A brave new world

'Create a sense of urgency. Even today, the pull of the status quo is so strong as to derail transformation efforts if urgency is not clear. Enough people at all levels of any organisation need to be convinced of the need for change or else the transformation efforts imposed can be slowed or sabotaged.'

'Leading Change, Ten Years Later', John Kotter, Professor of Leadership and Change, Harvard Business School

How much do we need to spend?

Late one Thursday afternoon I got a call from the CEO of a disability organisation, who asked me to give some thought to the question: *'How much do we have to spend on marketing in order to be sustainable under the NDIS?'* He wanted me to prepare something to present to him and a board member the following Monday morning.

I thought about it at length over the weekend. A series of recent interviews for this book had really influenced my views on what was actually achievable.

My answer surprised them both. I advised them that no amount of money thrown at marketing (or fundraising, for that matter) was going to be enough if they didn't change their business model. What was required was a strategic reinvention along the lines of a small business model.

What I've learnt from talking to families, clients and successful CEOs is that disability is a local business. In fact, it's the business of local community capacity building. Families don't want to travel. The typical disability customer is less mobile than the mainstream population and so less inclined to move providers or even move outside their local area to obtain support services. Local territory marketing and community engagement strategies are key business drivers.

The organisation needed to become sufficiently agile to respond to local customer needs and interests, and develop new service offerings compatible with their Mission and focused on their unique area of excellence.

Funnily enough, three weeks later I was asked the same question by another CEO.

Welcome to the new Australian disability sector

As I write this chapter there are over 2,000 disability providers in Australia who are facing massive internal and external change due to the introduction of the National Disability Insurance Scheme (NDIS) in June 2016. The first trial sites were launched in July 2013 in NSW, Victoria, Tasmania and South Australia, and a year later in WA, the ACT and NT.

Many smaller organisations, accustomed to block funding from government, are now at risk of financial collapse in the transition to a far more competitive, user-pays market for disability services. Around the traps, word is that many will disappear in the next 18 months due to closure or merger, as government funding moves away from block funding organisations to funding the individual requiring support.

The implications of these reforms for providers are widespread, as choice, control and buying power are transferred back into the hands of the individual with the disability (at last). This radically changes the fundamental dynamics of the market.

If the National Disability Insurance Agency (NDIA) does actually remove the current pricing restrictions (as it says it will at some time in the future) then, for the first time in our history, the disability 'market' will actually become a market as clients become customers who can directly purchase services of their own choosing, no longer the passive recipients of welfare.

With the pricing regulations as they stand, larger providers are at a distinct advantage due to their ability to more easily achieve economies of scale. The NDIA says it will allow an average over-head margin of 9%, which will make things extremely challenging for small providers with overheads averaging between 12% and 20%. The flip side is that smaller providers may be more easily able to innovate their delivery models, their services and organisational structure.

The bottom line is that, after decades of government depend-ence in this sector, many organisations now face the unfamiliar chal-lenge of being both 'mission driven' and 'market driven'.

To give you an idea of the scale of this upheaval: the 2,151 disability providers currently support on average 145 clients and employ, in total, approximately 70,000 people.[4]

As of September 2015, approximately 19,758 people with disabilities were accessing the NDIS in eight trial sites around Australia.[5] This number is expected to increase rapidly to 460,000 by July 2019 when the Scheme will be rolled out in full.

Spare a thought for the NDIA planners. In order to meet these targets, plan approvals must jump from 700 per month to 1200 per month by July 2016.[6]

---

4   NDS *State of the Disability Sector Report 2014.*
5   NDIA quarterly report, 30 June 2015.
6   NDS Annual Report 2014–15.

The great client scramble

For the larger organisations, the great client scramble has already begun as they move to acquire smaller providers in their drive to build client numbers as fast as possible. Despite their size, these organisations still have significant challenges ahead. They can invest in innovation, systems, training and quality support processes, however they still need a very different business model with significant new skillsets in order to control their costs, transform their internal culture and attract new clients.

Takeovers and mergers can raise massive internal issues, such as culture change, effective client communication, operational imperatives, staff assimilation, quality control and brand dilution. Economies of scale are not necessarily economies of quality.

For small providers this can be a scary time, but there is still plenty of good news. Over long years of relationships, clients and their families often become very loyal to their provider and especially to a single carer or therapist. So, what they need most of all is frequent, transparent communication about the changes that will affect them.

The early results from the eight trial sites indicate:[7]

- Most participants elected to stay with their existing providers.

- 19,758 people with disability now have an approved plan, at a total cost of $1.2 billion.

- The average package cost (excluding residents of large institutions) is $34,831.

- Participant satisfaction levels with the NDIS remain very high.

---

7   NDIS Quarterly Report Q1, 2015–16, 30 September 2015.

- 84% of registered providers are new to the NDIS.

- The most commonly funded supports comprise assistance with personal daily living activities.

- More work is required before the participant sees the NDIA planner. Even though 94% of NDIS applicants have been approved, only 57% of participants have had plans approved in less than 90 days.

Other conclusions include:[8]

- Building strong relationships between the NDIA, disability support workers, participants and their families and carers is critical to the success of the NDIS.

- Providers have become noticeably more customer-focused.

- Participants are exercising more choice.

This is a time for all providers to reach out to their market as they have never done before; attend the NDIA and NDS briefings; stay across the updates and reports; and talk to each other and their clients. Frequent communication and networking are critical.

Marketing is the survival catalyst

Now is the time for disability providers to do more than simply accept change; they need to actively pursue it. With the right business model and the marketing and business development skills to drive it, any provider can survive and thrive in this new landscape.

I believe that a simple shift in how the organisation defines their marketing function and how they then approach the opportunities out there right now will be instrumental in this success.

---

8   NDS *State of the Disability Sector Report 2015.*

I may be biased, but when you naturally see everything in terms of markets (or needs to be met) then everything becomes so much simpler.

Summary

▶ No amount of money will lead to sustainability if the business model is wrong.

▶ Disability is a local business. Families don't want to travel.

▶ The new funding model is the key strategic issue to resolve.

▶ The fundamental market dynamics have radically changed.

▶ Providers must be prepared to frequently reach out to their clients and each other to share information and learnings.

Interview with Gordon Duff, General Manager Policy and Research, National Disability Services

What are some of the major challenges facing disability organisations right now?

One of the major challenges facing disability providers is their preparedness and their ability to understand honestly where they are now. It's really all about senior management and Boards spending time revisiting their strategy and business plan.

This requires an assessment of their key capabilities: a diagnostic across domains such as leadership, governance, their embeddedness in their local communities, financial sustainability and being able to measure and demonstrate what they do are just some of the areas they need to look at, because a whole of organisation approach is required.

Affordable housing is one area of unmet market need; are you familiar with others?

- We know there are people who weren't previously known to the state agencies that will now be coming forward because the NDIS is coming to town. Whole new cohorts of people who were previously unknown to providers or the State government funder/administrator. In CALD communities, communication issues have played a factor in this.

- There's an enormous opportunity for those specialist service providers who have done the work to embed themselves in their local communities. 70% of NDIS participants will be people with an intellectual disability or cognitive impairment. And about 70% of what they will spend their money on is community and social participation. So, if you look at it purely in terms of where most of the money is going to go, it's not going to go to a specific service type or service, it's going to life opportunities. People won't say, 'I want this service'. What they will say is, 'I want a job' or 'I'm interested in these sorts of activities'. Unless you've done the work to be able to relate to life goals or interests and embed your organisation in local communities in ways that enable that interest to be satisfied, people will simply go somewhere else.

- There will also be new opportunities for providers offering more culturally proficient services. The UK experience saw greater industry consolidation, but also the emergence of new forms of start-ups for specific cultural groups. It was a case of people saying, 'We can't get it in the market so were going to do it ourselves.'

What would be your key message to disability providers with a turnover of $12 million or less?

This is a tough time for all providers. I'm not sure if I would have advice for an organisation based on size, but the obvious point is that everyone needs to get more efficient. The large organisations are carrying lots of layers of management typically associated with running programs. They now have to de-layer themselves because they're not managing programs, they are trying to respond to individual lives.

If the smaller organisations stay focused in the particular area that they're good at, and have the right partnerships in place, they could do very well.

What we certainly know, and this is consistent with international evidence, is that when people are given that choice and control they mostly turn around and go straight back to their same provider. In an uncertain situation, most people go with what they know. It will usually take a trigger, like something going wrong, before they think, 'Now might be the time to start shopping around'. In short, *providers will lose the business* by not listening intently to what people want, and matching diverse consumer preferences to diverse worker availability.

So, it's the same advice regardless of their size?

Up to a point. The problem at the moment is that the price is set, which means that economies of scale are more easily achieved if you're a bigger organisation. The agency (NDIA) has already indicated that they will deregulate prices and NDS advice is they should be trialling that now. There should also be other models of investment for innovative service providers to propose leading edge approaches that achieve defined, measurable outcomes more cost effectively (i.e. better than the average reference package, but share the risk and return with the NDIA as a commissioner and market steward). We are miles away from this more mature, more intelligent, outcomes-based commissioning. Instead, providers are competing on prices for some service types that are inefficient in that they actually crowd out innovation, and potentially compromise safeguarding.

Is it about being completely open to a structure change to deliver a service?

Yes, it's a complete whole of organisation change. A registered provider could be just one or two people or it could be a cooperative. In some trial sites it's difficult to see what's going on, simply because most of the organisations that are registering are actually sole practitioner allied health professionals. So what looks like lots of private limited companies registering is actually just one person.

Would you say that one of the primary target markets is future staff?

Yes. We know the workforce is a major challenge. In the disability workforce we have an ageing female workforce and it's completely out of profile with the participants, now and into the future. And in the future it's a reasonable assumption that people will go with people who are 'just like them'. The best organisations have already realised that they have to market themselves to employees first, so that when potential clients approach them they can say, 'You're a 40-year-old male whose just had a spinal injury, you're into x, y and z, we've also got a 40-year-old who used to work for a car plant and they have the same interests as you.' I'm talking here mostly about community participation. With respect to other service types, skills sets and experience, qualifications *are* equally important as worker demographics.

The NDIA planner is going to be a pivotal person in determining what supports can be included in that budget. Is that right?

For now, but not always. We've advocated for the position that choice and control should also extend to your choice of somebody to help you with your plan.

For some people, planning will be a straightforward experience because they know exactly what they want. Whereas for others, who have never been asked these questions before, and might have more difficult and complex needs, planning needs to be a much more iterative process, almost akin to a life coaching series of conversations. We could see some providers moving into that space because they may have already built up this expertise over the years. The reality is that most of the expertise about planning currently rests with service providers that interact with multiple aspects of people's lives. It will be a good thing to see planning become more independent of service provision and more specialised as a service in its own right.

How will quality be monitored?

By early 2016 COAG will receive advice on a framework, based on extensive consultation with stakeholders. The issues are so complex there will need to be transition arrangements to sort out which agencies are best placed to undertake each of the functions that taken together make up the preventative, corrective, educative functions and activities. The key is that there are a number of quality indicators that will emerge that consumers will trust and which, if they're not in an organisation's marketing, you will have missed the point entirely.

Are there partnership opportunities you would recommend for disability providers?

They certainly should be engaging in or considering partnerships. When I think about those partnerships, I think about it from the point of view of community embeddedness. It again comes back to the point that, if somebody comes forward and says, 'I really like gardening' or 'I really like swimming' or whatever, the provider needs to be in a position to say, 'Well, we have an arrangement with our local (gardening business/gym) and they're open to x', which may be work experience or employment or something of that kind.

Other partnerships between service providers can take many forms, and should.

Interview with Laura O'Reilly, CEO Fighting Chance

Australia has a very poor record when it comes to the employment of people with disabilities, ranking 21st out of the 29 OECD countries on disabled workforce participation rates.

In 2011, siblings Laura and Jordan O'Reilly launched innovative work opportunities for young Australians with severe disabilities through Fighting Chance, putting into practice their belief that every person has skills and abilities to contribute and deserves the opportunity to find meaning and purpose through work.

Over the last few years, Fighting Chance has developed two social enterprises that provide creative solutions to the complex problem of finding meaningful work for people with very significant disabilities. With a distinct service niche and a culture that embraces innovation and partnership, this disability organisation is well positioned for growth.

How did Fighting Chance begin?

Jordan and I had a younger brother, Shane, who was very severely disabled with cerebral palsy. We moved from Australia to the UK in 1995 so that Shane could access intensive daily therapy. My father was a senior political journalist and he gave up his career to be a carer for Shane. That was a really powerful influence in my life and Jordy's.

My dad died of cancer in 2006. He'd been the stay-at-home person in the family while mum had a demanding job as a journalist on Fleet Street. Mum brought Jordan and Shane back to Australia in 2008 but I stayed on in the UK to complete a degree in history at Cambridge University. When I returned to Australia a few years later, I was horrified at the lack of post-school opportunities available for Shane. I remember he was given a work-experience placement before he left school in a Disability Enterprise – previously known as a 'sheltered workshop' – but he couldn't physically do even the simple manual work on offer and it was made very clear he had no chance of being offered a place there post-school.

Shane however was a smart and ambitious young man who wanted to be able to contribute like his siblings. He was highly engaged, funny, and had significant computer skills. As someone who loved him and knew him, that's what I saw in him. Jordy and I were both really distressed to realise that there were literally zero work opportunities for Shane, as for so many other young Australians with similar levels of disability, and we were convinced that with all the business and work opportunities offered by modern technology and computers, there had to be some solution. So we began working at Fighting Chance in 2011 to change the number of opportunities available to Shane and young people like him.

Can you tell me about your two social enterprises?

Our ethos at Fighting Chance is that we believe in innovation and in creating innovative solutions to complex problems. The first problem we're tackling is the lack of employment and work opportunities available to people with complex disability in Australia. Our philosophy is that every single person has skills and abilities to contribute, and that no one should be left behind.

Avenue was our first social enterprise, providing training and vocational participation opportunities for people with profound disabilities. Avenue imports and sells products made by people with disabilities from across the developing world. We import these products and sell them online, at community markets and wholesale. The Avenue model is not about assembly or packaging. It's about online ecommerce. Avenue workers do everything from researching, contacting and communicating with global partners via email, through to choosing and ordering products, data entry, photography and selling products online and at local markets.

It took us two years before we were satisfied with the Avenue model. We tried many different things that all failed. We also made an intentional decision not to seek government grants or run government-funded programs, because we wanted to remain as free as possible to innovate and experiment in response to our day-to-day learnings, experiences and feedback from Avenue staffers. However, we partner with other disability providers and offer Avenue as a 'brokered' day-program service that provides technology skills to their government-funded clients.

Avenue is a partnership model that currently includes Cerebral Palsy Alliance, Ability Options, Sunnyfield, Lifestyle Solutions and Sunshine. The service is funded by the brokerage income. All profit made on the sale of goods goes to program participants through a profit-share model.

We're not trying to offer everything to everyone. Avenue's particular niche is offering work and vocational opportunities for day-program clients. We spoke to someone recently who wanted to get involved in bush regeneration as part of their day program and I thought, there's an organisation doing this so well just down the road, so we referred them.

Our second social enterprise, Jigsaw, assists people with disabilities who could and should be in mainstream employment but who are unemployed. This business provides outsourcing services to corporates and government agencies in the areas of document management and paperless office services. It also provides a transition into mainstream employment for people with disabilities. At present our partners include Warringah Council, Holroyd Council, Royal North Shore Hospital, a couple of corporates and a childcare chain.

In developing Jigsaw we realised that there were two things going on:

• Employers wanted to know that the people with disabilities could actually do the job; they wanted to see evidence of prior and successful work experience.

- People with disabilities often start work after a long period of unemployment, which means they often face anxieties about their new situation.

So we decided to develop a new business model, in between the unemployed jobseeker with disabilities and the general mainstream workplace. At Jigsaw, we first secure work contracts and then go out and hire people with disabilities to complete the contract in our work hub. We upskill our recruits by providing training, and we're able to absorb all that anxiety they usually have in their first few weeks on the job.

This is when the magic happens: when the person with the disability is fully comfortable and competent and a prospective employer has seen the outcome of their work and met the candidate, we then transition the employee into their new mainstream workplace.

The people who work at Jigsaw are paid from day one at a market rate. The business is funded by trade and by our own fundraising activities at Fighting Chance.

What impact has your Vision and your brand had on your culture?

I'm really conscious of how important the Vision is for our culture. We do a lot of work around creating an inspirational culture.

We have three brand values: *Excellence, The Power of Yes* and *Flexibility*. We need to do more work around articulating and documenting our brand and our culture, so that it doesn't rely on key team leaders. That's probably the next step in our maturity.

How important have partnerships been to your growth?

Partnerships have played a huge role. We've been lucky enough to be successful with grant applications from philanthropic trusts right from the beginning. It's been our lifeline; we've had amazing support from that space.

Our biggest partnership is the bike ride, the *Tour de Chance* that was organised by the father of one of our clients. He heard me speak at our annual Fighting Chance dinner in 2012, and he raised $50,000 on his own with a bike ride from Sydney to Brisbane. (What's been huge for us is the way our community has got behind our events.) This father just said, *'Right I'm doing something!'* And he called in favours and was successful to an extraordinary degree. He got all the sponsors on board for the event. We now say that the *Tour de Chance* has been the wheels of Fighting Chance. It's taken us from just surviving, which was the case up until 2012, to an organisation that could really grow. And it all sprang from just one advocate and supporter, bringing together the right people.

What's been the most successful marketing strategy employed?

The most successful marketing strategy is video storytelling, because we are putting together two concepts that don't often go together: work and vocational learning on the one hand, and people with severe to profound disabilities on the other. We have interns working very happily and productively at Avenue who many people would assume – and have in the past assumed – had no chance of ever being able to work. So we show videos of our guys working, so that other people with disabilities and their families can see for themselves what's possible. Expectations are so low in many cases; many parents don't believe their child can find meaningful work, until they see what others are achieving.

What are your growth plans?

Our goal is to open work hubs across the country, making the opportunities provided by Avenue and Jigsaw available to all. Within this model we want to structure our administration so that the business remains viable in the NDIS world and provides maximum value for our users. We plan to roll out hubs ourselves and through partnerships with other services. We're having amazing results in the community participation space with this enterprise model and we want to share that.

What do you think is the biggest challenge for the sector in preparing for NDIS?

I think the biggest challenge for the sector relates to innovation. I think we carry a responsibility in the coming years to get in and build new, completely different service models; not repackaged old models, but real innovation which truly meets customer needs.

With the NDIS's individualised funding model, disability service providers are going to have to attract people who want to buy what you're selling, so you have to develop innovative, genuinely effective programs that people will want to buy. Service providers haven't had to think like that in the past because pre-NDIS they received block funding from the government. I think the only way you will thrive under the NDIS is if you offer services that people will want to buy.

Chapter 2

Marketing (re)defined

This chapter is about how you define marketing and why this will make all the difference to your future success.

Definitions of marketing

I always start my marketing workshops with the question:

What do *you* think marketing is?

I've asked this question of accountants, mortgage brokers, scientists, aged-care professionals, social workers, doctors, disability service providers, cancer charities, and environmental and youth leadership organisations.

Interestingly, I nearly always receive the same answers – '*Marketing is:*

- brochures

- advertising

- social media

- the web

- promotion

- media

- PR.'

In a recent workshop a senior marketing professional offered the following classic textbook definition:

> **'Marketing is the management process through
> which goods and services move from concept
> to the customer. It's all about the four Ps:
> Product, Price, Place and Promotion.'**

While this *is* the textbook definition of marketing, it completely underestimates the human element: the personal relationships and the unmet customer needs and wants that are the key to an unbeatable marketing strategy.

Most people, like my workshop participants, define marketing by the day-to-day tactics and channels, such as social media, PR, advertising, direct mail and events. But this stuff is only the tip of the iceberg. It completely ignores the customer experience – the foundational stuff that drives strategic growth and generates long-term loyalty and financial sustainability.

If you're only focusing on the tactical then you're most likely wasting your money and totally underutilising the real power of marketing. We are social beings, and great marketing begins with understanding your customers' needs and wants and their problems *as they see them and as they articulate them.*

Purists may disagree, but for me, there's only one definition – from Peter Drucker – that absolutely nails it; that demonstrates itself to be true over and over again:

> **'Marketing is so basic that it cannot be considered
> a separate function. It is the whole business
> seen from the point of view of its final result,
> that is, from the customer's point of view.'**

When viewed in this way, marketing concerns every message your customer (whether a client, volunteer, donor, partner …) receives about your organisation as seen from *their* perspective. Every contact your organisation has with every stakeholder sends a message. (*For example: How do you answer the phone? How long do you take the answer it?*)

This is a much broader definition of marketing than you usually find. When defined in this manner, your marketing takes on an entirely new role within your organisation. Suddenly, your marketing activities can be extremely cost effective and highly targeted. Suddenly, there are all sorts of simple ways to successfully and cost-effectively market your organisation.

Where it all begins

At Amazon they call it 'Customer Obsession', and it's the first of their 12 leadership principles. They explain it in the following way:[9]

'Leaders start with the customer and work backwards. They work vigorously to earn and keep customer trust. Although leaders pay attention to competitors, they obsess over customers.'

It's no surprise then that Amazon is one of the largest, most successful retailers in the world.

Great marketing begins with understanding your clients or customers, knowing their problems and concerns, and reaching out to them in ways they are prepared to read, hear, feel and see. (Throughout this book you can interchange the term 'customer' for 'client', however it may actually be more helpful to start thinking of them as a customer.)

---

9   www.amazon.jobs/principles

From Drucker again: 'The aim of marketing is to know and understand the customer so well that the product fits him and sells itself.'

Great marketing strategy begins with your customer: *their* needs, not yours; *their* problems, not yours; and their wants (which may well differ to what *you* think they need and that's okay because *they're* the customer).

It begins with knowing things like:

- Who exactly are your current customers? How did they hear about you?

- Who are your ideal customers?

- How well do you know them? (Can you describe them without referring to your own services?)

- Why do they buy from you?

- What are their problems and unmet needs? (What do they really want? Think beyond the obvious and existing answers.)

Can you solve a specific problem for them better than anyone else? We will address these things in detail later. For now, I just want to underline the point that successful marketing begins with really knowing your customer. It does *not* begin with the services you wish to sell.

As a result, customer service has to become part of your cultural DNA: how you train your staff, the suite of service options you provide, and the way your team think, act and interact with every client needs to be totally customer-centric.

Your staff becomes your most important asset as the organisation's entire focus becomes the customer and the quality of the customer's experience with the organisation. This is about relationships and outcomes, not services and outputs. This is about equipping your team with the skills to enter into new customer conversations.

Marketing strategy and practice are in dire need of review across the Australian disability sector, and yet there are only a few providers addressing this issue successfully. (It's the sleeping giant, and there is this mistaken belief that you need a big budget to get it right.)

Achieving success within the NDIS landscape requires you to transform into a customer-focused business. You also need to clearly differentiate your services and articulate your value proposition; that is, you need to know what you do better than anyone else in your region, how to express that message, and how to promote it.

Once you begin to approach marketing in this way, once you can answer the questions above, your marketing strategy can be incredibly cost effective.

Then you can begin to move mountains.

Can you 'do' a brochure for us?

I often get asked this question and my response is always the same:

- Who are doing it for?

- What do you want to say?

- What do you want the reader to do after they read it?

- How are you going to distribute it?

If I receive blank responses to any of these questions, I suggest they get clear on their marketing strategy before they spend another cent on their marketing materials. It's too easy to waste money, energy and time on social media, PR, branding, brochures, advertising and the like if you don't begin with the foundational stuff: the market, your vision, your brand, your values, your target markets and your key marketing messages.

Marketing is everyone's job

If you adopt Drucker's definition of marketing then the marketing function can't just be left to the marketing department. Similarly, it's nuts to have a marketing department separate to a fundraising department. This is all about embedding the marketing function and your customers' experience (you can also substitute this with the donor or volunteer or sponsor experience) into the heart of your culture.

> 'It's everyone's job to tell the story of your cause in a way that will help others choose to get involved. It's everyone's job to create programs that outsiders can support. It's everyone's job to take part in the conversation about your cause. It's everyone's job to know, understand and respect donors.'
>
> *Jeff Brooks, Future Fundraising Now blog, '6 Signs of a well-run non-profit organisation', 2 June 2015*

Relationships, not transactions

This is not about making money or driving revenue. That will follow if you get this right. This is about the quality of the relationships you build with your clients, customers, donors and partners. It's about the difference they believe you're making in their lives and the lives of their families.

Your customers are looking for people who can solve their problems, and are prepared to – and *want* to – build long-term trusted relationships.

Your clients, their carers and families could become your most powerful advocates and ambassadors if they were totally engaged. This is so far removed from the typical definition of marketing; this is so much more relationship driven.

Your donors and supporters are also looking for something. They want to see the transparent results of *their generosity*. They want to get that *'I-made-this-happen'* impact in their lives, so you need to give the credit away generously and make them the hero in your stories. Individuals, businesses and organisations choose to support a cause because it says something to the world about them.

This is not about generating multiple transactions; it's about relationships. And before you can have a relationship you need to build trust. And before you can build trust you need to have awareness, and in the disability market nothing is more powerful than word-of-mouth advertising.

> 'Trust, it turns out, is not an event. You can't go from anonymity to trusted brand in a day. Instead it's a step-by-step process that requires time and money and commitment.'
>
> *Seth Godin*, Permission Marketing

This is all good news. Many disability providers have gained the trust and respect of their clients and their clients' families over years and years of reliable service. I believe that there is substantial unspoken, unleveraged goodwill out there just waiting to be tapped.

The photo competition that saved a coastline

Some years ago, I was working as a sponsorship marketing consultant for a national environmental organisation. After nine months of trying to find a sponsor for a four-wheel-driver awareness program I had one prospect left – a well-known car company. They had already declined two different submissions for the same project. I then discovered that the CEO was a photography enthusiast. This simple fact changed everything. I prepared a new submission – and suddenly we had a sponsor.

With photo competitions in every state (the CEO was on seven judging panels), we created a massive free image library that still promotes the cause today. We secured free vehicles, national outdoor advertising, educational pamphlets, and a massive financial three-year commitment. The campaign also won a national promotional advertising award for the sponsor (which they loved).

The lesson is this: very often, securing a great customer, partner, sponsor or donor has very little to do with you at all. It's all about them.

Marketing and Mission – is there a trade-off?

For the more traditional disability organisations, decades of dependence on government funding have meant that they have not had to look elsewhere for their financial viability.

As a result, anything vaguely commercial can sometimes be seen to be 'at odds' with the rights of the individual with the disability to access the best quality support. I've sat in meetings where senior management are clearly uncomfortable at the mere mention of the words 'marketing' or 'fundraising'.

But let's go back to the heart of the industry phrase 'person-centred': surely this means that everything begins with the client, their needs and wants? The same is true for great marketing: everything begins with the customer. If your Mission is highly relevant to the needs of your existing and future customers then there is no trade-off.

Summary

▶ How you define marketing makes all the difference.

▶ Great marketing begins with knowing and understanding your customer, not the services you want to sell.

▶ If you're not clear on your marketing strategy you may be wasting your money on your materials.

▶ Marketing is everyone's job. Think relationships, not transactions.

▶ Smart marketing doesn't need a big budget.

▶ Being Mission-driven and market-driven isn't a trade-off provided your Mission is still highly relevant to your customers' needs.

Interview with Aviva Beecher Kelk, Clickability

Aviva Beecher Kelk is Co-Founder and Director of Clickability, a rating and review website for the disability sector which launched in April 2015. Her team's goal is to provide a platform through which the disability community can obtain reliable information about support services in order to make informed choices and decisions. She is a social worker and a PhD student with a background in mental health, community development and project management. Aviva is passionate about creating person-centred social change through community engagement and social enterprise.

How did you get involved in the disability sector?

I was studying my masters of social work and working in mental health and found there was a distinct lack of information about the quality of services available in the sector. I found that I was the one who held all the information. I was the one talking to providers about what they were offering and finding out whether it would fit a particular person's need. My business partner Jenna is a social worker with experience in acquired brain injury. She was finding the same issues. There were so many service directories and none of them had any really meaningful information. So every time we had to make a referral we were ringing up our colleagues to get some first-hand knowledge about which services were good.

It was not just that there was a distinct lack of transparent information; it was also the fact that service providers were talking about what they were *doing* rather than what they were *achieving*. We wanted to help providers find a way to articulate some of the amazing things they were doing in a way that was meaningful to consumers. It's about explaining things like, *'How have I supported this person? What have they been able to achieve as a result of that? What's my evidence base? As a consumer, what am I actually purchasing when*

I'm purchasing this service?' Finding a way to articulate those issues prior to the customer making a purchase is very important, the same as it would be in any other industry.

The uni project I was doing at the time was about program planning, and I focused on the NDIS because the launch had just been announced. I planned this huge mobile multidisciplinary allied health clinic and had a one-liner in it about a consumer-rated service directory. Jenna was proofreading it for me and she said, 'Oh that's a good idea! We could do that! It'd only take us, like, six months, right?!' Yeah, *right.*

How does the mental health sector overlap with disability?

That's a big question. There was some debate about whether mental health would be included in the NDIS, but everything is pointing to that happening. Diagnosing mental illness can be difficult in the first place, and making assumptions about what the diagnosis will mean is also difficult. It's called 'psychosocial disability' for a reason – the social aspects are just as important as the psychological ones. Regardless of the diagnosis everybody has varying needs. The NDIS is fairly straightforward for people with static, physical disability, however it presents challenges for those people who may go in and out of illness or have different needs at different times. People who have been diagnosed with schizophrenia or bipolar often have those periodic illnesses.

How do you fund Clickability?

It's a subscription-based service. At the moment we're working with a freemium model in the Barwon area. We've uploaded every provider who is registered as a service provider in the launch site. They all have a listing that can be rated and reviewed. If they want to add their branding and obtain data about who's been looking at their listing then they can pay for that extra functionality and access. We have a few other ideas but that's where it is right now.

What are your growth plans for Clickability?

Our next stage is to launch across Victoria, and we will move to the other launch sites after that. There's something to be said for launching ahead of the NDIS and working with the local agencies. We'd like to be in another state in the New Year.

Have you based it on any existing platform overseas?

We didn't initially, but since launching we found a few similar platforms. Our favourite of all of those functionality-wise is SENDirect in the UK.

Do you have any competitors in Australia?

There are quite a few service directories but no one else is doing the rate and review thing yet. Our consumers are the only ones who do the rating and the methodology is quite transparent.

How important is the Clickability brand to your growth?

We've gone out of our way to create a very clean brand that doesn't have any acronyms in it! It's person oriented, and young with a casual, friendly tone. We're political with a small 'p': we're all about empowerment and advocacy, but we want to do it in the same transparent, consumer-driven way as Trip Advisor or Yelp. We're not a charity, and we want to see the disability industry move away from the charity model. We want to see the purchase of disability services normalised – yes, this is still a human rights issue, but you know, I can't fix my own car when it breaks down, I need someone to help me with that; others can't get out of bed and need someone to help with that. There should be no stigma, and there should be just as much of a consumer-driven information economy available. We have clear values that underpin our brand: transparency, authenticity and passion. We also try to keep a sense of humour – people keep telling Jenna and I that we're both pretty funky, light people, and our team certainly laughs a lot.

How important have partnerships been to your growth?

We're all about partnerships, that's where it starts and ends. There is a feeling in the sector there which is a little 'us and them', whether 'them' are consumers, or service providers, or the NDIA. And we're all about connecting and collaboration. I feel so comfortable with the fact that we've positioned ourselves right in the middle of service providers and consumers – we all want the same thing at the end of the day!

We have an extensive network of mentors and advisers who are passionate about helping us professionally and personally. We have informal partnerships with individuals, peer groups, advocacy groups and service providers – all sorts of people. There are groups from the medical sector, social work, psychology; people from policy backgrounds, researchers, government and corporate.

We've just won a $10,000 award from Macquarie Bank through the School for Social Entrepreneurs. We've also received sponsorship from Go Get and another couple of corporate sponsors who haven't given us permission to name them as yet.

There are some lovely people in the philanthropic grant space who would like to support us but can't because we are not a registered charity and don't have deductible gift recipient status. We have deliberately not become a charity because of wanting to normalise disability support, and this problem with being able to access funding is a real symptom of society needing to catch up with social enterprise models providing innovative solutions in spaces where charities have traditionally sat.

What's been your most successful marketing strategy?

We actively talk with stakeholders in the community, go to consultations, ask for advice and genuinely connect with other individuals who are actively involved in community development. We're social workers, you know, and our marketing is community development – with lots of face to face and social media.

We also have staff members who are volunteers and disability advocates in their own right. That's been huge for us. Each of us has used our own networks and passion to help us build our community.

What do you think is the biggest challenge for the disability providers and the NDIS?

In the Barwon launch site they actually call it the 'new world'. It's such a different system! Change is really hard. I know I keep coming back to this, but the charity mindset is really interesting and problematic in this transition. When you have a block of money given to you, you know exactly what you can afford to do, and you measure your success by measuring your *output*. There's no growth mindset, because it's literally not an option. Even in the Barwon launch site two years on there's still not enough supply to match the demand. It's a paradigm shift to restructure for growth and start measuring success via *outcomes*. Not to mention developing meaningful, targeted marketing material. As a sector, we need real-time monitoring and evaluating around customer needs and whether those needs are being met. We need to develop sensitive measurement tools to monitor outcomes around growth and recovery as well as customer satisfaction, because they can be two very different things!

Also, holding onto cooperation is important, even in the face of competition. If you're an agency that provides A and C services, and B is just not your game, that's fine, but having an arrangement with another agency that does provide B is going to benefit everyone at the end of the day. There's still a human rights imperative here, it's still public health. Let's start talking about 'coopetition'.

Funding is another immediate issue – even if there's a good transition plan, moving from a block-funding model into the NDIS will take a lot of reserve for the big agencies, and a lot of them won't have access to it. Most of them can't borrow money because they're not-for-profit. There's a lot written about how funding limitations could impact the workforce too in terms of training, qualification, and casualisation.

Another problem is bureaucracy. The bigger agencies will have to become leaner, firstly for funding purposes – the NDIS pricing has been calculated on a 7% to 15% overhead, which is very low. They'll also have to move very quickly where a lot of them are used to lengthy decision-making processes which involve their boards – another symptom of not-for-profit culture. But it needs to shift if organisations are going to be able to respond to the needs of their customers with flexibility.

How do you promote more risk tolerance on the part of everyone in the sector, including the NDIA?

In social work we talk about 'dignity of risk'. If consumers are going to be making their own decisions then surely they can take their own risks to some extent. There needs to be that balance of dignity of risk – the freedom to make decisions even if they're 'the wrong' decisions. There was a beautiful blog written on our website a few weeks ago that defined the right to choice as: 'an individual has meaningful options, is given accessible information, is supported to make a decision, and has that decision respected.' I'm really talking about that last bit, of having the decision respected. A fair bit of the work that Jenna did as a case manager was advocating for people to have their decisions respected by their friends and family. We don't know yet what the NDIA Safeguarding and Quality Assurance framework will look like, but it will be really interesting to see how they respond to the challenge of duty-of-care versus choice-and-control! I'd love someone to develop a Risk Tolerance Index. Maybe that's the next project!

If you had a message for disability providers what would it be?

Be brave. Be brave in taking risks and be brave in planning space and in articulating value, in being unique and making friends and embracing 'coopetition'.

Chapter 3

The Seven Steps to Sustainability

'Develop your transformation plan and establish the guiding coalition.'[10]

Embracing change

I'd like to share with you an exciting meeting I had this week.

The purpose of the meeting was to discuss the project management of an annual report. It was with the CEO and two senior managers of a $6 million community services organisation which had begun its life nearly 30 years ago. Like many others, they currently receive over 90% of their funding from government.

Over the last three years they had been going through massive internal change. But they were so connected. They were a team, with strong mutual respect, lots of eye contact, and they were passionate about their clients' personal achievements and the impacts the organisation was having in their local community. It struck me that here was one of the best examples I'd seen in a long time of Kotter's 'guiding coalition': *'The right team, not just the top players, is still a must for effective change to happen'.*[11]

---

10 'Leading Change, Ten Years Later', John Kotter, Professor of Leadership and Change, Harvard Business School.

11 Ibid.

There was a distinct willingness to embrace change. The CEO said he was looking for 'the glue' to bind all the pathways of change together. He wanted a step-by-step process that they could move through and 'tick off' on a monthly basis – a single, robust framework that would bind his team together, create excitement as well as urgency, and facilitate the transformational change required for NDIS.

I asked if they had a marketing plan. Despite their size, there was no marketing manager or clear marketing strategy. I then explained the idea of strategic marketing: how marketing can be used to drive strategic growth and organisational change. How a strong brand can be used to build team alignment around the vision and connect new clients, donors and partners to their cause. This is not just piecemeal change delivered via a marketing plan; this is transformational change across the organisation driven by the brand. And I gave examples of some of my other clients who had followed this process.

The Seven Steps to Sustainability

I then realised that I had just run through my own 'seven steps' yet again, for the umpteenth time in eight years. These steps work for me. There may be faster pathways, but the change may not be sustainable. This is about long-term relationships, not quick wins. From experience, these seven steps build strong, enduring relationships that, if managed correctly, gain momentum and drive growth over the long term.

The NDIS requires whole of organisation transformational change, not just a shiny new marketing or fundraising plan. If implemented successfully, the seven-step framework delivers brand-driven transformational change.

Why you need a guiding coalition

Change isn't easy. It means being prepared to let go of what's familiar and moving outside your comfort zone. It requires courage and frequent, transparent communication, with lots of face-to-face time to build team trust and share the vision.

If the senior management team is not already 'connected' and willing to change then my model will probably create fallout. It forces managers to be accountable for outcomes within specific transparent timeframes, and for some, this can be challenging.

These seven steps assume you already have in place your own 'guiding coalition' and a CEO or a senior manager with the ability to provide visionary leadership. If the organisation is highly siloed and poorly led then this will be a tough road with a doubtful destination.

The purpose of **The Seven Steps to Sustainability** is to provide you with a pathway to long-term financial sustainability. The framework has been designed as a highly practical step-by-step guide to help organisations handle the massive changes required by the NDIS and transform from a community-based charity heavily dependent on government funding to a mission-driven, customer-focused non-profit.

The model uses the brand as the 'glue' that binds the organisation internally and externally to all key stakeholders as it navigates transformational change.

The diagram on the following page outlines the seven steps which we will cover throughout the rest of this book.

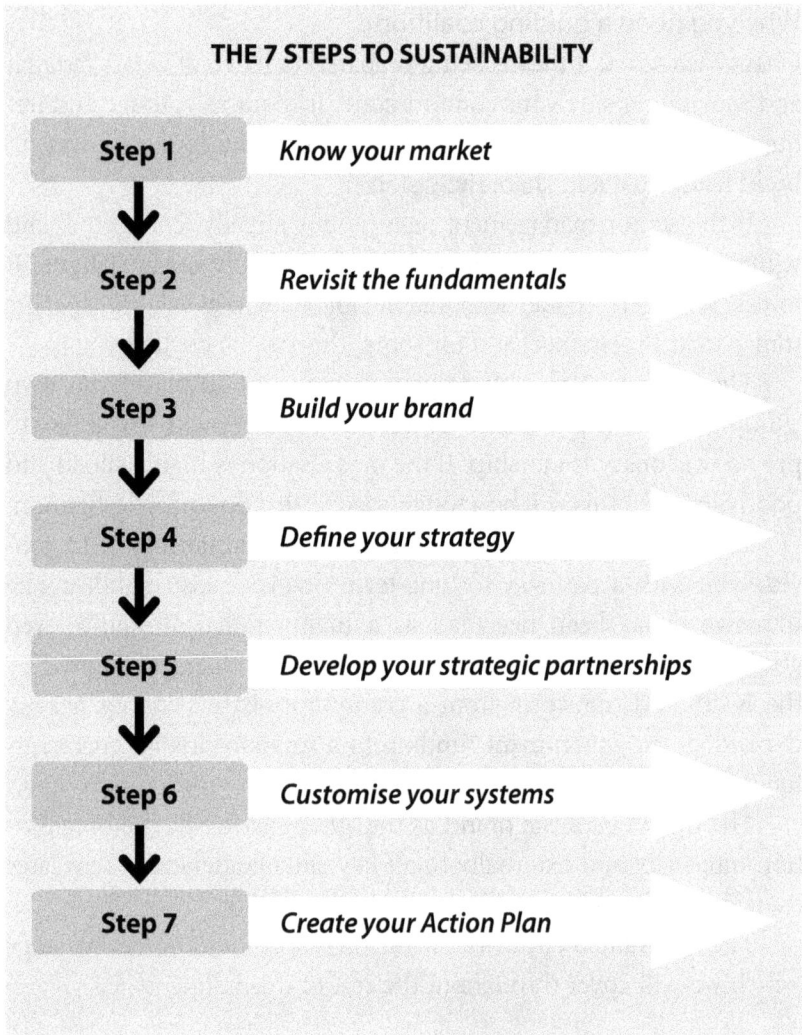

THE 7 STEPS TO SUSTAINABILITY

Step 1	*Know your market*
Step 2	*Revisit the fundamentals*
Step 3	*Build your brand*
Step 4	*Define your strategy*
Step 5	*Develop your strategic partnerships*
Step 6	*Customise your systems*
Step 7	*Create your Action Plan*

Summary

▶ The NDIS requires whole of organisation transformational change, not just a new marketing or fundraising plan.

▶ You need a clear strategic direction and visionary leadership to drive transformational change.

▶ You also need your 'guiding coalition' of a connected, committed senior management team.

▶ *The Seven Steps to Sustainability* model is a purpose-built, brand-driven model that facilitates transformational change in non-profits.

Chapter 4 ► **Step 1**

Know your market: this is not about you

'I have learned, based on my experience, that everything is dominated by the market. So whenever we are struck with any obstacles or difficulties, I always say to myself: "listen to the market, listen to the voice of the customer". That's the fundamental essence of marketing. Always, we have to come back to the market; back to the customer … We really cannot determine anything. The customer does that.'

Yoshio Ishizaka, Executive Vice President, Toyota Motor Corporation

The disability market in Australia

Despite the fact that I've used the term 'disability' market in the preceding chapters, the truth is that there is no one disability market. The disability sector comprises several different markets that vary significantly in structure and maturity.

The vision impairment market differs from the hearing impairment market which differs from the supported accommodation market – and that's just for starters.

The fact is, there are simply too many different 'disability' markets to address them all individually. But, no matter what market you work in, there are fundamental principles that apply to every market, so you should be able to find some information of use in these pages.

On 16 September 2015, bilateral agreements for the roll out of the NDIS in New South Wales and Victoria were finally signed. It is expected that nearly 245,000 people will ultimately be covered by the Scheme in these states. To give you an early indication of the funds involved, currently the average annualised package cost (for these states, excluding residences in Stockton, Kanagra and Colanda) is around $33,357 per person.[12] Bilateral agreements with the other states and territories are still to be finalised (and some early transition sites in Queensland have been confirmed).

There is no doubt that the NDIS is the ultimate market disrupter. The implications of the most significant reform in the history of Australian disability services cannot be underestimated. In this chapter we look at the big picture, and then drill down to the key target markets that will directly determine your ongoing sustainability.

The stats

- The NDIS will increase the number of people who receive support nationally from 220,000 to 460,000. Disability spending will increase nationally each year from over $7 billion to $22 billion by 2020.

- 18.5% of the population, or 4.2 million Australians, have a disability.[13]

- 45% of Australians with a disability live in or near a state of poverty.[14] This is more than double the OECD average of 22%.[15]

---

12 NDIS Quarterly Report, 30 September 2015.
13 Australian Bureau of Statistics, 'Survey of Disability, Ageing and Carers: Summary of findings', No. 4430.0, ABS, Canberra, 2012.
14 PwC, 'Disability expectations – Investing in a better life, a stronger Australia', Canberra, 2011.
15 Organisation for Economic Co-operation and Development (OECD), 'Sickness, Disability and Work: keeping on track in the economic downturn', Background paper.

- 2.7 million Australians provide informal care to an older person or person with a disability, with 29% of these people identifying themselves as the primary carer.[16]

- In 1993, the labour force participation rate for working-age people with disability (15 to 64 years) was 54.9%, and dropped slightly to 52.8% in 2012. During the same period, the participation rate for working-age people without disability increased from 76.9% to 82.5%.[17]

- People with disability are twice as likely to be in the bottom 20% of gross household incomes.[18]

- Nearly 40% of Australian non-profit organisations receive 75% or more of their total funding from government.[19] (This average is much higher for disability organisations. Over the last two years alone I've worked with clients who receive 64%, 85%, 90% and 98% of their total revenue from government.)

Research by the National Disability Services (NDS) stated: '*It would be counter-productive to drive out good not-for-profits if all they lack are resources and skills to market their services.*'[20]

The same report found that the current disability research base is fragmented and not fit for purpose. Other key findings included:

- In 2012–13, 312,539 people received funded services and the average expenditure on disability support services per organisation was $3.3 million.

---

16 Australian Bureau of Statistics, Survey of Disability, Ageing and Carers: Summary of Findings. No. 4430.0, ABS, Canberra, 2012.

17 Australian Bureau of Statistics, 4433.0.55.006, 'Disability and Labour Force Participation', 2012.

18 Australian Bureau of Statistics, 'Survey of Disability, Ageing and Carers', 2012.

19 'NFP Benchmark Survey Report', March 2015, Russell Kennedy Lawyers and Pitcher Partners.

20 NDS, *State of the Disability Sector Report 2015.*

- There are 2,151 disability support organisations in Australia, with an average of 145 'service users' and 27 paid full-time staff members per organisation.[21]

- A few organisations reported they were NDIS-ready on costing and pricing (20%) and marketing practice (21%). These were the two areas where those surveyed were least prepared.

- 67% of organisations did not have the minimum recommended cash flow standard of three months or more spending reserves. 17% had a current debt-to-assets ratio of less than one.

- 70% of providers intend to increase the scale or range of services.

- 42% of small providers believe the risks of the NDIS outweigh the opportunities.

All the data points to increased consolidation, collaboration and partnerships within the sector: 26% of disability providers are now working in joint arrangements.[22]

The big hairy challenge

The Australian disability sector is undergoing intense change and rationalisation. This is generational change the likes of which we haven't seen since the introduction of Medibank (now Medicare) in 1975. It appears to me that this change is being driven by three separate but related issues: the National Disability Insurance Scheme, the rapidly increasing demand for services, and the ageing population.

---

21 The ACNC Australian Disabilities Charities 2014 Report stated that 11,528 charities helped people with disabilities in 2014 and 64.1% of those were less than $250k income. This included all charities, not just those delivering disability services.
   Source: www.australiancharities2014.acnc.gov.au
22 NDS Essential Briefing, August 2015.

The overwhelming challenge for many providers becomes one of successfully achieving transformative change at the same time as whole of organisation operational change. It is difficult to separate the broad range of interconnected issues that lie beneath this.

For simplicity's sake, I've split these issues into the following key problems:

1 *Understanding the customer:* Everything now begins with the customer, not the funded service line. This places the typical disability model on its head. It means that many community-based organisations must for the first time think and act like a customer-focused business.

2 *The cash flow gap:* Under the new NDIS regime, it will be the client who receives the funding not the organisation. This has significant workforce planning and cash flow implications as funding will be paid in arrears rather than in advance.

3 *The funding gap:* The NDIA pricing structure does not cover many of the organisational expenses critical to the quality of the service, such as staff training and professional development. This funding gap requires new operational efficiencies across the organisation and a far more diversified funding base.

4 *The unit costings:* Providers now have to know and really understand their unit costings in order to remain financially viable. They also need to test different costing scenarios around the expected client funding package.

5 *Fewer players:* There will be increased industry concentration due to new partnerships, mergers and takeovers. The need to collaborate is greater than ever before as providers face the fact that they can no longer be the sole provider of everything to their customer, nor can they achieve efficiencies without scale.

6   *The talent hunt:* There will be increased competition for talented, experienced staff at all levels of organisations, but particularly in senior management as new skills are required.

7   *Increased competition:* Providers with larger marketing budgets will more actively promote their services and new commercial providers will enter the sector attracted by the new client funding.

8   *Cultural challenges:* There will be significant shifts in the nature and composition of the disability workforce. This presents major internal cultural challenges; for example, as you're now in the business of 'life outcomes' not services, is your workforce age appropriate and 'a lifestyle fit' for your customer? Does this mean a casualisation of your workforce? How do you embed a customer-centric ethos if your organisation is split into functional silos?

9   *Strategic challenges:* Issues such as a strong differentiated brand platform and an integrated fundraising and business development strategy are critical for financial sustainability. In the current landscape, this requires visionary leadership skills. How do you identify your ideal service niche and create an entrepreneurial mindset that is consistent with your Mission? How do you identify the partnerships you need for long-term financial sustainability? How will the organisation's fundraising capacity be affected if their donors think the NDIS has 'the problem sorted'?

10 *Systems integration:* The challenge becomes how do you successfully implement and integrate the back office and frontline systems required within the timeframe available? For example, how do you manage a QMS with a casualised workforce? How do you deliver a seamless CRM with mobile-enabled frontline workers and new Position Descriptions that enable sufficient autonomy?

In the absence of strong visionary leadership providing a clear strategic direction, these hurdles may well be overwhelming. Things like unit pricing, delivering individually tailored services within a quality management framework, and funding the cash flow gap between what the client pays and what it actually costs to deliver quality services are major challenges for all providers.

Big and small face different challenges
Many of the large providers will be well positioned to manage the financial challenges ahead; however, they face the challenge of removing layers of administration from their organisation resulting from decades of block funding. Organisational silos will make it very hard to create a culture that embraces change. Larger providers may find it difficult to truly innovate in response to customers' needs. It will also be harder for them to target a clear and distinct market niche.

For some smaller providers the financial hurdles will be overwhelming. For many, the loyalty and goodwill they may have from many years of reliable service provision of high-quality supports in a specific location will be a security. However, they still need to manage the significant financial issues presented by the new funding model and the NDIA pricing.

The small providers may well have the long-term advantage, provided they can survive the NDIA pricing structure and build a financially sustainable business model that is successfully marketed to a clear niche.

The new opportunities
With an ageing population, rapidly increasing demand for disability services, increasing competition from commercial providers and a full-scale national rollout of the National Disability Insurance

Scheme scheduled from June 2016, now is the time for disability providers to reach out to the market like they have never done before. The NDIS brings significant opportunities for providers who:

- clearly identify their niche within their region and are prepared to be different and do things differently

- no longer see themselves as providers who deliver programs

- innovate by creating new products and services that deliver specific life outcomes

- rearrange their business model entirely around their customers

- collaborate, cross-refer and partner with other organisations (NFPs, corporates, small business and sole traders).

What research do you need?

The absolute first step in any great marketing strategy is market research. Imagine for a moment you're a small business owner in the health support services market and you were thinking of expanding your business into a new territory. There is a wealth of local information that you're going to need before you can make sound business decisions. It makes good sense to draw a circle around your current geographic footprint. Then you take a microscope to that market and gather as much information as you can.

Here are a few ideas to get you started on your research:

1 Market demographics: projected growth, age mix, cultural mix, health status and disability profile, etc. This data is readily available from your local area health website and from the Australian Bureau of Statistics.

2 Review your competition: their pricing, services, locations, strategic goals, revenue, staff numbers, geographic footprint, history, management, business structure, marketing activities,

and the calibre of their local reputation and their staff. Ask your clients who they perceive as your competitors; don't assume you know and don't assume it's another disability provider. Once you have a list of key competitors you need to understand how they describe their services, the key messages they use, how they position themselves. In the retail world 'comparison shopping' is done all the time. An easy way to do this is to get on their mailing lists, or set up a Google Alert to monitor your competitors and industry trends.

3   Identify your current and potential clients and referral sources.

4   Identify your current and potential partners. (What allied services exist in the area that might be a logical, 'mission-fit' partnership with your business?)

5   Where are the greatest areas of unmet need? What are the new market opportunities that already exist because nobody else has listened sufficiently to the unmet need? For example, is anyone currently offering a range of lifestyle choices to your clients? This could be things like further educational, employment or hobby pursuits that go *way outside* any previous offering to cater for the goals of the individual. How bespoke is your service?

6   Who are the key local influencers in your area? The small business owners, the school teachers, the allied health workers, the GPs, the local politicians, the media outlets, the Rotary Club, the Lions Club, the service clubs, etc.

Identify your key target markets

Before you can begin to develop an effective long-term strategy for financial sustainability, you need to know your key target markets like the back of your hand.

As I said before, disability providers can't expect to be all things to their clients. It's just not healthy or practical. As in any successful small business, you need to know – really know – where you excel in comparison to the competition. (This is the only way to find your ideal niche, and we cover more of this later in chapter 7.) But before we get to your niche, there is a practical starting point that simplifies and fast tracks the planning process. I usually find that the five key target markets to address are:

- current staff

- current customers and their families

- future staff

- future customers and families

- current and future partners (you could include referral networks and donors here).

Just hold that thought for now. We're building a Marketing Action Plan. I will return to these target markets shortly.

Disability is a local business

I cannot overstate the importance of having detailed first-hand local market knowledge. You need to live and breathe your market, because under the NDIS disability will become a local business.

Families don't want to have to travel to find the services they need. Convenience, high-quality supports and customer service will be key business drivers. This is a huge opportunity for small niche disability organisations with entrepreneurial skills. The smaller you are, the more agile you can be!

As a result, you need to be aware of the emerging trends inside your client base, inside your own network of families, and inside your community. Be prepared to experiment and think beyond traditional disability services to meet the needs of the families and individuals you serve.

Summary

▶ The current market challenges require clear strategic direction and visionary leadership.

▶ There are huge opportunities for the agile and entrepreneurial.

▶ Do your market research.

▶ Know your local market and the competition like the back of your hand.

▶ Service providers can no longer be all things to their clients.

▶ Disability is a local business.

Interview with Janet H, Parent

Janet's daughter Georgia was born 28 years ago with mild intellectual disabilities. Janet and her husband were told that Georgia would never attend school. Thanks to considerable early intervention, Georgia was able to attend mainstream schools. Following a traumatic episode at the age of 15, Georgia was diagnosed with mental health issues.

In 2009 Georgia was one of the first people in New South Wales to receive an individually funded package. Initially this was brokered through a large service provider but now the family have been able to achieve considerable savings by directly managing the funding themselves. Georgia leads a rich and varied life, studying art and Roman Architecture at Sydney University through the Centre for Disability Studies. She lives independently, volunteers regularly, is an accomplished artist, has a personal trainer, and is a very popular and familiar face within her local community.

Can you give me some background to Georgia's story?

Georgia is a twin. She was the second born and it was a breech birth. We were not aware of any problems until Georgia was 19 months old, when she was not walking or making any progress. At the age of two we had her assessed and were told that she would never attend school; that was devastating.

So we went to early intervention and began physiotherapy, occupational therapy, speech therapy. We decided to forget what we'd been told or accept the prognosis, and we booked into Montessori where she had a brilliant teacher. She then went on to mainstream primary and high school and did amazingly well until, at the age of 15, she was bullied at a school camp and experienced very serious mental illness.

The wheels started to fall off as diagnosis was hard to achieve, puzzling teachers, medicos and social workers. We finally found a pediatrician who told us Georgia was psychotic. There was nowhere to take her and she ended up in a medical ward at Westmead Children's Hospital. She was terrified by the hallucinations. As a family we took it in shifts to stay by her side for three months until we were finally asked to leave because the bed was needed.

She was still 15, and our only option at that time was an adult psychiatric hospital. They were mixed wards and we were concerned about her security. When we raised our concerns with our case manager he responded in front of my young son by saying, 'She won't be a virgin forever.' It was incredible.

So we were stuck with nowhere to send Georgia. Eventually we found a place that agreed to take her on a daily basis. She had a really nice, caring teacher but she was in a class of children with extreme behaviours which was very challenging. Georgia stayed there for a year and then transitioned to a high school with a special disability unit.

They didn't blend it well. Unlike the mainstream schooling Georgia had been used to, she was now treated as a person with a disability within a special unit. She had a variety of work experience roles (which were hardly suited to her). In hospitality she was breaking cups all the time. She was then placed in a restaurant where her only job was to cover baking trays with glad wrap all day. She had to be there by 7 am every morning. It was crazy; the supervisor in the kitchen was very tough. It was too much pressure on her and she began to get unwell again.

(If you're placing people with disabilities into hospitality roles, put them on the front desk of a hotel, don't hide them in the kitchen! Georgia loves talking to people.)

It's worth looking at the types of work for young people with disabilities. At TAFE, Georgia was making beds for a year and the boys were panel beating which were both difficult and quite dangerous.

Then she went to a local service provider who soon lost their funding. We were offered an alternative provider, but there was nothing there that was appropriate, so I rang ADHC (Ageing, Disability and Home Care) and they asked me if I would like to go onto a new self-funding package through a large disability provider based in Penrith.

This was a gift.

We set up a meeting, and invited a close group of friends and family to be in a circle of friends for Georgia. We just put charts on the wall and brainstormed about what Georgia would like to do, what interests her, and we began looking at how we could get Georgia to a better life.

She wanted to get healthier, she wanted a personal trainer, and she wanted to study art. So we took these three things to start with. That's how a new world opened up for Georgia. Since then she's illustrated two books, she's won art competitions, she's had lots of success and it's all improved her confidence.

These days, it's hard to believe she's the same person. She does a lot of volunteering work. She has a whole cupboard full of volunteering T-shirts. She has three days a week at Sydney University where she's doing screen printing and studying the history of Roman architecture. She has her personal trainer two days a week and she loves going to the movies. Georgia has a really rich and varied life.

What would be your message for disability organisations?

I think they get hung up on the disability thing. As we've shown with Georgia, these are people who can make a contribution so we need to start recognising their ability. That's how you build rich and connected lives. We need to recognise what people have to offer and not pigeonhole them because they have a disability.

Georgia had very early mainstream experiences, so she doesn't want to be in an environment that consists solely of people with disabilities.

We've all got things that we can't do but we're not labelled. Disability is seen as a stigma that you have to carry. It's not just a change in language that's needed; we need a change in mindset.

Providers need to think beyond delivering services to enabling lives. If they can begin to think like that there's lots of opportunities to support people who want to live independently:

- Families with adult dependent children who need to get their kids out into independent living.

- Support workers who can also be companions of a similar age. At uni Georgia is supported by other university students and she loves it!

- Many people will have no idea how to allocate their NDIS funding and will need advice. That brokerage space is also a place for providers; however, it will be a shame if people have to lose funds from their package simply to make an informed decision.

How do you hope the NDIS will work?

One of the best things about the NDIS is that it will be supporting people who have never had any funding before.

I hope we will be able to continue with the same arrangement as Georgia has right now. Georgia's funding now comes direct to her rather than going through a service provider. They need to understand that this means she has more to spend on her support needs. It took six months to process that change and now we can allocate it to everyone she uses.

We don't know how this will change if we have to go through an NDIS planner and frustrating assessment. I think our biggest problem is that we've taken Georgia to such a high level that they will assess her as a high-functioning person who does not need any help.

We can only keep Georgia at this level because she has the funding she needs. If Georgia's package was withdrawn she would just go backwards; she would be back in hospital. It's a long recovery and a big drain. If support was removed it would only increase the cost to society and negate the funds already spent.

It's hard to imagine that the person that she was at 15 has become the beautiful, happy young woman she is now at 28. It's been a journey. As parents we were very determined, because we were in a very bad place. We thought we understood the intellectual disability, but we had no idea that mental illness might have been even a possibility and what it would put us through.

It's very complicated and confusing around the different government funding entities. I can't get my head around it, so what about people who don't have English as a first language? I don't know how they manage.

Interview with Libby Ellis, CEO InCharge

Libby Ellis is the Founder of InCharge, an organisation that supports the efforts of people with disability to create a life they can call their own. This is about big vision, raising the bar on what is possible, and being in charge of your supports and funding.

Her brother, Matthew, is a man with significant intellectual disability who doesn't speak, yet with the help of family and supporters he lives in his own home with non-disabled people, has his own niche business and organises his own supports and funding.

Can you tell me how you became involved in the disability sector?

In my early 20s I started to see the paucity of my brother's life compared to mine. Apart from us, he was surrounded by people who were paid to be there. He grew up in group homes, attended special schools – it was a prescribed life. Towards the end of Math's schooling nobody asked, 'What could life look like? What does he want to do?' They only asked, 'He'll be going to XYZ, won't he?'

Two things occurred to me in my early 20s: what must it be like to live a life surrounded by people who are paid to be with me? And secondly, what would it be like to have no say in who I spent my time with?

I then went and worked for advocacy organisations and developed a strong understanding of how people feel in the system. I saw at one end the embattled, disrespected, 'case managed', tired, taken-for-granted and ignored. At the most serious end, I saw regular occurrences of abuse and neglect.

My personal and professional life put me in touch with many local and international leaders who challenged and questioned this, who sought more, who believed that people themselves could determine what they needed.

One of the common themes was their belief that different things could happen for someone if you built supports from the basis of an individual; their uniqueness, their culture, their personality, hopes, fears and dreams, and the specific support requirements emerging from their disability.

I wanted to do something around change. I felt driven to create something that aspired to be alongside people in their own efforts at change. In my work I noticed there was a gap between having really exciting ideas for your life and knowing *how* to make those ideas come about. InCharge helps people with these 'hows'.

As a family member of someone with a disability, how do you think the NDIS will affect your brother and your family?

Money doesn't make ideas happen. The vision must come first. NDIS in itself is going to be an enormous national bureaucracy, but for me it must also be an opportunity for people to transform things for themselves.

Matthew already has an individually funded package and he directs the use of those funds with the assistance of a wider network of family and friends. We're very fortunate that he is living a life of his own choosing – being really disabled but having an experience of working through a micro business, travelling, living with non-disabled housemates and having friendships with people who aren't just paid to be there.

I would like to think that the NDIS could help Math sustain his own supports via:

- *Workforce participation:* We want Math to continue to have his own life so that he doesn't have to depend on us all the time to get things off the ground. So when it comes time for life development stuff like building his business or just maintaining it, it's not up to us to do it. So having some resources to continue to build his economic participation and independence.

- *Ageing:* Our parents are going to die. Fact. My younger brother and I will become more responsible for Matthew's support. But we have families and lives of our own. We are talking about how the NDIS might support Matthew to grow his networks so that we can all continue to have our own lives and care for each other, but not depend wholly on each other.

- *Collective supports:* We've always desired to join with others who share our values. I would like to think that the NDIS would enable Math to join a collective that allows for a cooperative sharing of resources, responsibility, ideas and support.

How do you think our language must change around disability?

There are so many different aspects to this question. It's such a big conversation. We must be careful about the stories we tell about people. And frankly I think this is a question better directed towards someone with a disability.

When we use the word *choice*, how do we enable someone who is already marginalised and has significant disabilities to exercise choice? There is a self-actualising piece missing before someone in this situation can truly be said to be empowered to choose. What choices do people get offered? When my parents were offered schooling choice it looked like a school with a pool, built-in therapy, 1:1 support, small classrooms. Versus local mainstream school with … well, a hell of a struggle. That is no genuine choice. So we must be careful when we use this language that it has substance behind it.

We also need to think about the terms *client focused* and *customer focused*. For most of us we're clients or customers in only a smallish proportion of our lives. For people with disabilities their whole life could be a life of 'client hood'.

Language is so fundamental. The term *service* is currently used to describe services delivered by providers. The transformative idea of *service* for me is that the service delivered is not an end in itself; it's the means to an end. It's just one vehicle to a more equitable citizenship for people with disabilities.

What we're after is a more inclusive Australia. A country where you routinely see people with disability and have some kind of relationship with them; for example, they were at your church. They were employees. They served you in your regular shop. They ran a business you used …

In your opinion, what's the number one thing disability providers must do to become more client focused?

Form ethical partnerships with people with disability and families that build the foundations for self-direction. That means trust. It also means devolving authority. An organisation is a collection of authority that has been delegated – from the Board to a CEO to Managers, direct staff and even volunteers. It is possible to delegate authority to those that use the service to undertake roles and responsibilities. We've had these kinds of partnerships with disability providers. We've taken responsibility for hiring and managing support workers, for example. The service has helped us learn these responsibilities and tasks as well as be the legal employer of the staff. They've stuck with us when times were really tough. So what we were always seeking was someone who was prepared to partner with Matthew, to be on his team.

How do you hope the NDIS will change the sector?

The National Disability Insurance Scheme brings not only significant change in financial investment in people with disabilities, but also enormous opportunity for how people get the support they need.

It would be so fantastic if we could have a broad cross-section of innovative new services, including those run by people with disability themselves to serve themselves or a small group of likeminded people. Organisations and services which provide the pathway and transition points between the old and new, like InCharge does. There are more of these initiatives starting, and I hope the NDIA genuinely supports this emerging sector. The task for these organisations is to create a collective voice and action around this.

If you had one key message for disability providers right now what would it be?

Yes, people need direct services – therapy and workers and equipment and personal care and assistance with daily living.

But every one of us, even if we are not able to articulate it, has a sense of what we want to do with our lives, as well as what is missing and what we need. Disability providers need to be able to facilitate those conversations, and facilitate, resource and help people to take action on their own solutions rather than trying to be *the* solution.

People with disabilities are going to need partners, and this is a new role for disability providers. It's a new form of service, one without bricks and mortar or white buses but one that could really be about transformation in people's lives.

Chapter 5 ▶ *Step 2*

Revisit the fundamentals: your Vision and Mission

'Never doubt that a small group of thoughtful, committed citizens can change the world; indeed, it's the only thing that ever has.'

Margaret Mead

Once you've done your market research, you can begin to turn your attention inwards and consider the foundational stuff for long-term sustainability.

Your Vision and your Mission lay the foundation for your strategic plan. If your goal is to create a financially sustainable, customer-focused non-profit, then your Vision and your Mission must be relevant to the needs of your future customer.

What is a Vision?

An organisation's Vision is the ultimate statement of its ideal future state. It should encapsulate what the organisation aspires to achieve and become. It's the destination that will guide your strategy.

It is, by definition, focused on the future. It must be relevant to the likely needs of your future clients or customers, and it should be distinctive compared to your competitors.

A word of warning: some organisations spend weeks (even months) debating single words in noble-sounding statements.

However, if you don't get team 'buy in', these words will be meaningless. The Vision needs to be created in a way that provides engagement, involvement and meaningful direction. The process you use to develop the Vision will make a massive difference to the quality of the outcome.

Vision Statements are not just token words on a page. Nor are they statements to be crafted by committees inch by inch, word by word until they've lost all passion and meaning. If you get it right (both the words and the process) then your Vision can seriously fast track your financial sustainability.

The best Vision Statements are:

- focused

- easy to understand (people need to get it right away)

- inspirational

- vibrant and compelling

- timeless.

Sample Vision Statements

- Bill Gates' original Vision for Microsoft: 'A computer on every desk and in every home.'

- Honda: 'We are a company built on dreams. And these dreams inspire us to create innovative products that enhance human mobility and benefit society. We see "The Power of Dreams" as a way of thinking that guides us and inspires us to move forward. The strength of our company comes from this philosophy – based on the visionary principles of our founder, Soichiro Honda.'[23]

---

23   http://corporate.honda.com/about/

- Amazon: 'We seek to be Earth's most customer-centric company for four primary customer sets: consumers, sellers, enterprises, and content creators.'[24]

The importance of a shared Vision

A shared Vision is a tool that helps you align the organisation and create the future. When people feel connected to the Vision it creates a synergy that encourages and promotes change and growth.

In Stephen Covey's book *The Seven Habits of Highly Effective People*, Habit 2 is 'Begin with the end in mind'. He states that all things are created twice. He writes:

'If you want to have a successful enterprise, you clearly define what you're trying to accomplish … The extent to which you begin with the end in mind often determines whether or not you're able to create a successful enterprise.'

Habit 2 is all about leadership. To extend Covey's metaphor, it's the leader who determines whether you're actually in the right jungle before you start cutting down trees. Leadership comes first, then management.

It's not good enough to have a framed Vision Statement over the reception desk. You may as well have a painting on a wall. Every member of your team needs to know and understand where you're heading. They need to feel personally connected.

I once ran a Visioning workshop for a large aged care provider. Their Vision Statement was framed in every reception in every outlet of their organisation. However, nobody except the CEO could repeat it unprompted. Following the workshop, not only could everybody repeat it – they owned it! They were part of the team that would make it happen. It had, finally, become their Vision.

---

24 Amazon Investor Relations http://phx.corporate-ir.net/phoenix.zhtml?c=97664&p= irol-irhome

A few months later I was thrilled to receive a call from the CEO. He sounded so enthusiastic on the other end of the line, and quickly blurted out: *'Fran, I just wanted you to know, your workshops have made all the difference. People are excited again! They're committed, they're being creative, they're solving problems and I really feel like they're all on board!'* The lesson for me was to never underestimate the positive impacts that flow from achieving team alignment around the Vision.

Why you need visionary leadership

During my time in the non-profit sector I've seen leaders who manage, leaders who lead and then a few leaders who actually provide visionary leadership. In times of massive change, it's the third category that's most needed.

Now, more than ever, leaders in the disability sector are being tested. With the changing funding model, many CEOs are under the kind of pressure they've never seen before to lead transformational levels of change.

Visionary leadership inspires change in others by sharing the Vision (and the reason for that Vision) with frequent and transparent communication, firstly with your team and then with clients, families, partners and the community.

It's about sharing a meaningful image of the future that will resonate with each of these groups. It requires a clear communications plan across the entire organisation.

Visionary leaders know how to share and how to listen. This is the antithesis of the outdated 'command and control' style of leadership. A shared Vision is owned by everyone in the organisation. Command and control leadership won't get you to sustainability.

What is a Mission?

A good Mission Statement answers these questions:

- What do we do?

- What is our purpose?

- Who do we do it for?

- Why do we do it?

It describes the organisation's reason for being or its purpose.

Your customers don't buy *what* you do; they buy *why* you do it. So if you or your staff can't articulate why you do what you do, how can you (or they) possibly sell your services?

Inspiring others begins with knowing your why. In his groundbreaking book *Start with Why*, Simon Sinek remarks:

> **'If the leader of the organisation can't clearly articulate why the organisation exists in terms beyond its products or services then how does he expect the employees to know why to come to work?'**[25]

Sinek gives the example of 20th century English explorer Ernest Shackleton's advertisement in the *London Times* which he used to recruit his team:

'Men wanted for hazardous journey. Small wages, bitter cold, long months of complete darkness, constant danger, safe return doubtful. Honour and recognition in case of success.'

Shackleton was ensuring that every applicant believed in the Mission of his expedition. He was specifically recruiting for 'cultural fit'. Despite being stranded in the Antarctic for ten months, losing their ship *The Endurance* and being stuck on the ice, no one died.

---

25 Sinek S, 2011, *Start with Why*, Penguin Books.

Finding a cultural fit within an organisation gives meaning to work and enables us to define why we do what we do. It also gives the organisation a much stronger chance of survival.

In the non-profit sector it's often easier to know why we come to work. Social impacts are often more visible, more real. Dedicated staff very often forego market salary rates because of their passion for what they do.

The Mission Statement: Cerebral Palsy Alliance[26]

This is a great way to construct a Mission Statement – combining the values within the Mission actually serves to reinforce the internal organisational culture.

Cerebral Palsy Alliance is committed to providing world-class services for people living with a broad range of disabilities, and their families. As an organisation we embed our values of Integrity, Passion, Excellence, Courage and Respect in our practices every day. We are here to make a difference in people's lives and support them in connecting and engaging them with their communities.

Where does it all fit?

The Vision Statement says where you're heading (*the destination*). The Mission Statement says why you're heading there (*your purpose*). The organisational strategy lays the path (*the how*).

It's too easy to overcomplicate organisational strategy. From experience, the simpler and more consultative your processes are, the more likely you are to get traction. There are umpteen different ways of approaching strategic direction; unfortunately these models ebb and flow with the trendy model of the time.

---

26 www.cerebralpalsy.org.au/why-us/

Having worked in the corporate, small business and non-profit sectors I think we can learn a lot about strategic leadership from small business. (Nothing focuses your thinking like your own money on the line!)

I spent many years consulting to small businesses: accountants, mortgage brokers, property developers, testing laboratories and financial planners. It was here that I developed my own processes for creating a clear organisational Vision that generates strong team alignment.

Together, the Vision, the Mission, the values and the brand form the foundations for a clear strategic direction.

Linking your Vision with your cause

'It's been 67 years since a small group of parents gathered together to establish this organisation, formerly known as the Handicapped Children's Centre NSW. It was their vision to create a world where children with disabilities could lead the best possible life.'

Sylvanvale Foundation Annual Report 2014

So many great disability organisations began their lives in this way. Their origin stories reflect a strong entrepreneurial spirit responding to the immediate needs of local families. This is the kind of spark of energy that attracts people to your cause and finds new funds on a shoestring budget.

Once you've articulated your Vision and ensured that your Mission is market relevant, you can begin to draw a line from the very beginnings of your organisation to the present and then into the future. This means you can begin to tell a powerful story that illustrates how today – more than ever – your organisation is client focused and Mission driven, and how tomorrow you'll be making an even greater impact in the lives of the individuals and families you support.

Today, donors, mummy bloggers, joggers, cyclists, corporate partners and countless other groups rally around 'causes' that deliver transparent social impacts, rather than organisations that fundraise. It's a critical shift in the fundraising mindset. (People don't give to you; they give *through* you to the cause.)

With several notable exceptions, it's fair to say that non-profit organisations outside the disability sector (with far less government support) learnt this lesson decades ago. Amnesty International, the Fred Hollows Foundation, the Heart Foundation and the RSPCA – to name just a few – are master communicators and fundraisers for their cause. Successful non-profit marketing and fundraising is not about money. It's about meaning and belonging. It gets back to who you are, what you stand for and how you share that message. Building and leveraging a great brand is the secret to unlocking hearts, minds and markets.

In the next chapter we look at the brand as the catalyst for organisational change.

Summary

▶ A Vision Statement encapsulates the organisation's ideal future state.

▶ A Mission Statement explains why and for whom. It's the reason you exist.

▶ The process you use to create the Vision Statement makes all the difference.

▶ A shared Vision creates team alignment, attracts support and achieves incredible traction.

▶ Never underestimate the power of a shared Vision.

▶ Times of change require visionary leadership.

▶ 'Command and control' leadership won't lead to financial sustainability.

▶ Tell powerful stories that link your cause and your Vision.

▶ People don't give to you; they give through you to the cause you represent.

Interview with Rob White, Chief Executive Officer, Cerebral Palsy Alliance and Elise Stumbles, General Manager Strategy & Development, Cerebral Palsy Alliance

Cerebral Palsy Alliance (CPA) provides family-centred therapies, programs, equipment and support for people living with cerebral palsy and their families in 55 sites across NSW and ACT.

The organisation has over 1,000 staff who support approximately 4,000 clients each year. Over the last year, 85% of their workforce completed customer service training as part of a broader internal change management program. CPA is open and collaborative in their approach to creating partnerships and sharing knowledge in order to improve the outcomes for people with cerebral palsy. Last year through their RTO, CPA trained 5,428 people from 60 disability organisations.

Unlike many disability service providers, CPA has a highly sophisticated fundraising and marketing department and, not surprisingly, a strongly diversified funding base. They are crystal clear on their Mission and their brand is a stand-out success in the crowded Australian not-for-profit sector. CPA is also the largest non-government funder of cerebral palsy research in the world. They are planning to increase their fundraising revenue by 100% over the next five years.

Rob White has been CEO of Cerebral Palsy Alliance since 2000. Elise Stumbles is a registered psychologist who began working with CPA 14 years ago. Her diverse portfolios include strategic planning, oversight of their RTO, innovation and talent management. Elise is leading CPA's participation in the NDIS trial sites in NSW.

How did CPA begin?

Rob: The organisation began back in 1944, when Audrie and Neil McLeod put an advertisement in the *Sydney Morning Herald*. Their daughter had cerebral palsy and they were looking for other families who needed support. Together with eight other parents they purchased a house in Mosman. The Spastic Centre, as it was then known, was the first organisation of its type in the world for people with cerebral palsy.

What are some of the major challenges facing disability organisations today?

Rob: Firstly it's mission, it's scale, it's lack of business know-how and expertise, and the need to hire the right staff. The biggest issue at the moment is the changing funding model. So cash flow and balance sheets are key issues.

How is CPA helping individuals and families understand what the NDIS will mean for them?

Elise: There's been a couple of key activities that we introduced from the start. Firstly we offered information sessions to clients and families on a monthly basis around the state. They've been really successful with between 23 and 70 clients and families in the room depending on your location. We felt it was important not to speak for the National Disability Insurance Agency (NDIA) but to share with our clients what was happening for us, for their services, how we'd be supporting them with the transition into the future, and point of them in the right direction so that they could get the right information about the scheme and the agency. We've continued to do that and the program is now in its second year.

Another new thing was that we realised very early on that families were very anxious about their planning meetings with the NDIA and were circling back to us for support. There was a lot of anxiety from families who were trying to ensure that they would not lose anything. We quickly responded and set about offering families support in preparing for their planning meetings.

Over time the planning process is becoming more efficient and effective. Once the planners realised that as providers we had really valuable information to input into the planning process, it made it easier for all stakeholders involved. We've since produced an online booklet which we keep developing in response to what families find helpful and it's had a huge uptake.

While it's potentially easy for someone to have a conversation around their broader life goals there's a lot of gaps missing around daily issues such as pain management, equipment needs and their physical health. There are a lot of things that are quite specific to the nature of cerebral palsy where we can add value and support for our clients.

Our clients' nominees and guardians were very happy to have us involved in the conversation because quite often we had more information than they did.

What have been some of the major learnings out of the trial sites?

Rob: You need to be prepared to work closely with the NDIA and share learnings. Everybody in the NDIS is there for the right reasons.

This is a trial and we are all trying to learn and be open. We've learnt a lot around process. Initially in the Hunter we had two group homes each with 10 people in them and everyone had a different planner. It wasn't particularly practical. We've learnt that the time-lines the agency have and the timelines the family have are often not the same. Families may take up to two months to sign a contract. They also tend to stay with the providers they know.

We also learned that you have to get your own house in order. There are many ways in which disability organisations can be more productive, more efficient, and deliver a more streamlined service, especially within the therapy area where a portion of what we did in the past will now have to be covered by our own fundraising activities (for example, research into early diagnosis and early intervention prior to diagnosis).

We've worked very closely with the NDIA to say that sometimes kids won't have a diagnosis but you need to fund children at risk because the outcomes will be far greater if we do this. The NDIA understood that if you can intervene at three months then you can reduce the lifetime expense.

Elise: One of the key learnings for us is that the NDIS puts real pressure on your business systems and processes. Most of our business systems were developed with the government as the customer. That required an enormous transformation for us. Our HR, Finance, CRM and CMS systems all now need to focus on the actual client as the customer.

That's not only an investment in technology, it's also an investment in the right people to do the data analytics. You need the right people to interpret that information to support the frontline staff who actually use those systems. We still have a fair way to go, but we've got a plan over the next 12 to 24 months to really ramp that up.

How did you support your workforce to become more customer service focused?

Elise: We've had to come to terms with the fact that being 'customer centric' is quite different to being 'person centred'. When you apply a commercial lens to your client relationships you uncover a lot of stuff. You can't underestimate what that really means. Broadly speaking, our sector has become 'person centred', but trying to take that culture and expect your workforce to also become 'customer centric' is a different thing.

It takes quite a degree of effort to support everyone with that shift and still maintain your mission and your values. The question becomes, 'How do you bring the best of commercial reality and remain true to your mission as a not-for-profit charity?'

We're halfway through a massive internal change management program. We've hired a customer service consultant to come in and work with our teams. Our goal is to get 90% of our staff through the program, and so far we have 85% through, or 800 staff.

We've used the program as a way to reach everyone and say the NDIS is coming, this is what it is, this is why we need to change, this is how we need to change, and this is what we need you to understand. We also shared with them what the organisation needed to improve on in terms of processes and systems.

We were able to get huge engagement by bringing in clients to share their personal experiences with us. They shared what was going well with their interactions with us and what wasn't. We shot videos of a range of clients who were so eloquent around their needs. They were very loyal but my goodness there are some things that we were doing that made it really hard for them.

We are only on the cusp of this, and we've learnt that unless we provide a lot of coaching and support to all the middle managers it falls over. We're all in this together. We've got high engagement at the moment and everyone feels really supported. But it's early days. The driver now is customer satisfaction; it's not outputs for government.

What advice do you have for providers with a turnover of $12 million or less?

Rob: There is a significant role that smaller organisations can play in supporting local families. They have a big advantage in that they can be niche and local, but they really need to work out what services they do and don't want to be in.

There is going to be so much work for all providers. The issue will be choosing the right services to deliver. This has to be the work you do really well, where you can actually say you're one of the best. In this way, everybody wins. The client wins because you're very good at delivering this service, you win because you can put a margin on it, and the agency wins because they can demand a fair price. If we can all sit in that sweet spot then everybody wins.

Other disability organisations are not the competitors. The NDIS is a $22 billion funding envelope; the largest disability provider in NSW has a turnover of $400 million (Life Without Barriers). Our turnover is $100 million. So this is a huge, amazing opportunity for all service providers.

Partnerships are really important. It makes sense to draw a ring around your geographic footprint and then work out what other organisations you can partner with and then cross refer expertise.

There's probably a few other things you need to consider here:

- Get a good chairman and a board with business acumen and a real understanding of the NDIS.

- Understand the cost of the business and understand what kind of margin is right for your organisation.

- If you can find good people at the right price they can add so much value. There are many things that people feel they have to have in house but we find we're using more and more consultants.

Elise: I think financial sustainability is the single most significant strategic issue. It really does depend upon the individual organisation and what services they develop and deliver and what differentiates them. From a working capital perspective, I think it's vital to start planning out how you will manage that. You need to really focus on what you can do better than the competition.

I also feel that effective communication internally and externally is really important. We've recognised that the NDIS is a massive reform and that everyone is learning. So we've tried to be genuinely positive and optimistic externally and internally. Behind the scenes we've developed a really good communication mechanism with the NDIA at a local level to support clients of families. For me, it's all about relationships and good communication because these are essentially the things that will help you achieve major change.

It gets really hard when you're a bigger organisation. We have a senior staff meeting of 120 senior people from all over the state every eight weeks where the CEO gives an update. That cascades around the organisation. Those sorts of things are incredibly important.

How important to you are partnerships?

Rob: Being open and generous is part of our organisational culture; we've always been willing to share anything with anybody. If you go back to our Mission, the Mission is for people with cerebral palsy, it doesn't say we have to provide everything for them. We want the best services for people with cerebral palsy; if that means we need to train other people we will.

CPA is an RTO and we train about 60 other organisations. If there's a client in Orange who can't get a service from us then we're very happy to make it a good service from somebody else.

I think we need to be clear about language when we say merger or takeover. The organisation is not here to employ us; it's here for the client. I do think partnerships, mergers and takeovers are essential for organisations that don't have the business software.

Partnerships can work in complementary ways; we do therapy, they do accommodation. That's what the 'for-profit' sector does really well. Clients will want to experiment as well and we will have to accept that. It's quite unhealthy if you've got one person with the one provider all their lives meeting all the needs. The fact is that until now, there hasn't been a huge choice for people and that's been the issue.

How important is your brand?

Rob: We consciously changed our name so that it's really clear what we're about. Brand is critical. We talk about our values a lot here, without sounding corny, and we chose values that reflected the things we all believed in. We also give out staff rewards based on those values. We certainly recruit based on value fit and we're trying to get more sophisticated with that.

We have a full-day orientation that kicks off our six-month induction program. In the first part of the day we talk about our values and we get our best people to run it. It's around setting context, explaining where we come from, explaining that we were started by passionate parents and that passion is one of our values.

As an organisation we really do strive to embed our brand values of Integrity, Passion, Excellence, Courage and Respect in our practices every day. I'm proud to say my team lives by these daily.

Have you gone down the path of starting a social enterprise?

Rob: Everybody now calls themselves a social enterprise. I worry about terminology when everyone jumps on the bandwagon. I sometimes think it's just rebadging. I get what it's all about and I do think there is a future there but I don't think Australia's there yet.

We split our high-performance staff into three groups and we gave each group a six-month project. One of them was how to become more productive as an organisation, another one was around how to get the right workforce, and the third one was about how to protect our social capital as we move into an NDIS world.

We will explore social enterprise but our core focus is not going to be that. We now lead the world in cerebral palsy research. This is an area where we prefer to focus our energies. We're also identifying other markets that we want to play in. We employ more therapists than anyone else in Australia outside of government. We pump a lot of our discretionary funds into therapy development as well as research. It's all about responding to market needs rather than pursuing funded services.

Interview with Steve Scown, Chief Executive, Dimensions UK

Steve has worked with Dimensions UK for 23 years and has been Chief Executive for 4½ years. Prior to becoming Chief Executive, he led the development of Dimensions' response to the personalisation agenda and co-authored the award-winning book *Making It Personal*.

Dimensions is one of the four largest disability providers in the UK with a turnover of £110 million. They support 3,500 people with 5,000 staff in 500 locations across 75 Local Authorities. Their work is entirely funded by local government authorities who 'commission' services on behalf of clients.

How would you describe the UK disability and social care market?

There are three groups of care: children, working-aged adults and ageing adults. There is a distinct difference between each of these groups, between the older person's social care market and other parts of the market. We work primarily in the disability sector supporting adults with learning disabilities and autism.

The learning disability sector has been shaped by the history of institutional closures of the late '70s through to the early '90s. There is a significant not-for-profit element in this market. There is also a significant number of very small for-profit providers and local charitable trusts. There are some very large not-for-profits like my organisation, and you have small regional ones and large for-profits with national footprints. So it's really a mixed bag. For people with extremely high complex needs there is a further complication where the individual may be funded both by social care and by health. (And it gets very confusing for everybody.)

In terms of the older persons market it is far less diverse with a more significant for-profit presence.

What has been the impact of the larger commercial providers like BUPA, Serco and Virgin on the quality and pricing of support services over recent years?

In the UK, BUPA tend to do private healthcare and older people services, Virgin just do health. Serco has very little, if any, social care to any material extent in the UK. Currently commercial organisations mainly focus on the self-funded older persons market.

Then you have a different tranche of for-profits who focus on the working age disability sector, venture capital funded complex structures like Voyage, CMG and Priory. Priory are the largest for-profit provider in the UK. They work in mental health, disability and substance misuse. These for-profits focus on high-cost complex needs services, price accordingly, and make a stonking profit. You do find some not-for-profits in this area but to a lesser extent.

The for-profits have a very distinct problem-solving offer: the problem they solve is urgent need and they deliver a resilient, robust service. They have a much more holistic model: psychiatrists, psychologists, therapists, and they charge for it. The not-for-profits' offer is narrower and often they can't respond immediately.

How are people coping with being given their own funds to spend in the UK?

There are a small proportion of people who want to exercise control over their own money, so they will seek out a personal budget and become a family 'Commissioner' of services. The vast majority of people don't want the hassle, so they basically allow the local authority to act as their 'Commissioner'. So we have a situation where the local authority is the economic purchaser and you have the family who are the emotional purchaser, and you have the provider in the middle trying to meet the needs of both. You can have a lot of tension between the two different buyers. The family could become the direct employer themselves but it doesn't happen very often. You have to have a family with a lot of energy and resilience to take on the hassle of managing staff and coping with the required bureaucracy.

What would be your message to Australian disability providers facing the NDIS?

We've had to learn to cope with continuous environmental and organisational change. So it's about being successful because we've been prepared to experiment and try something new. We've also been prepared to make decisions about what we are not prepared to do. So we've become much more focused over the last six years.

The most significant cultural shift we have had to undertake is to recognise the importance of working positively with families. Six or seven years ago personalisation was coming down the track and we said we've got to become more family friendly. We had hundreds of staff who basically kept families at arms-length. We had to recognise that that was an unsustainable cultural characteristic of the organisation. We knew we had to become more family friendly.

In your opinion what are the key ingredients for financial sustainability for a smaller medium-size non-profit provider?

Be really clear about what you're good at, be really clear what your customer wants and get as much of both of those to be the same thing as possible. There's no point being really good at something if nobody wants to buy it.

I think one of the challenges for the UK not-for-profit organisations is helping their trustees or Directors understand some of this stuff. Here you have lots of long-standing 30- to 40-year-old charities that were set up to do something that nobody else was doing at a time when funding was more generous. Their trustees have deep-rooted loyalty to their longest standing services. The problem is that many of these services are just not wanted any more. It can be very difficult for trustees to accept that what they were founded for is no longer relevant or financially viable.

If you were a small provider and you've identified what you're great at and you've matched it against the customer's need, how do you still make it financially sustainable?

Again it comes down to basic economics. You've got to be prepared, willing and able to think beyond the current delivery mechanisms. It's about saying just because it's worked in the past doesn't mean it will work in the future, and being prepared to have that honest conversation with your workforce and your trustees.

How do you maintain continuity and quality of care with an ageing workforce?

I think this will be one of our major challenges in the future, far more than it has been. You need to get your recruitment right to begin with and be very honest with new employees about what the job is and what it isn't. You need to have senior leaders who are prepared to deliver tough, honest and sometimes unpleasant messages and who are prepared to get out there, meet people and listen.

We've also looked at what's worked in other industries. It's about making sure that your workforce is engaged and that you pay as competitively as possible, so we benchmark ourselves against other industries.

We make a great deal about using person-centred tools and the value of work that is actually giving someone else a fantastic life. We do a lot of matching. For example, if we have someone who loves photography we will try to recruit a landscape photographer to support them. So we really try to find ways of allowing people to do what they like to do anyway while working for us.

How important is the brand to your internal culture?

Our values are very important to us and are inherently within all our materials. Our annual staff awards are based upon living and exhibiting the brand values and we always try to express our values in a way that fits with our audience. For example, one of the values

is 'Courage', so we expect our staff to be courageous when supporting an individual and when working with their family. So we try
and help our staff understand what they need to do in very different
scenarios based on the brand values.

It all comes back to leadership. There cannot be a disconnect between leadership behaviour and organisational behaviour;
you can't expect the support worker to be courageous if the Chief
Executive isn't.

What role have partnerships played in your growth?

'Partnerships' is a word that has a lot of different meanings and
can be very confusing for people. There is a big difference between
working alongside another organisation in a collaborative partnership and having a partner.

We cannot be everything to anybody, so we work hard at collaborating with providers of other services in somebody's life. We also
work in partnership with families, so you can cut the word 'partnership' in many different ways.

We have one partnership with a legal agreement, a joint venture
with another charity, Ambitious about Autism, and we've created a
new school. This is a formal partnership and it is very different.

What are some of the key lessons that might apply to Australia?

Knowing what I know now my top four would be:

- know what people want and know what you're good at –
  and get as much of that on the same page as possible

- be prepared to say 'no' more often

- work positively with families

- be humble, and be prepared to say sorry and admit when we
  got it wrong.

Chapter 6 ▶ *Step 3*

Build your brand: spread the word

'The essential difference between emotion and reason is that emotion leads to action while reason leads to conclusions.'

Donald Calne, neurologist

Driving your brand

A strong brand acts as a declaration of what you stand for, now and in the future. In the commercial world, a strong brand is a central platform for a clear market position, a dynamic communications strategy and a high-performance culture.

Your ability to build a strong, overarching brand strategy will significantly impact your entire organisational strategy. It requires consistency in design, messaging and structure.

The average Australian non-profit brand is outdated, misunderstood, undervalued and underutilised. As a result, too many non-profits fail to successfully leverage the power of their brand to unite, promote and raise revenue for their organisations.

Many Australian disability providers fail to successfully leverage the power of their brand simply because they haven't had to; they've had one (reasonably guaranteed if they did the paperwork) customer for years: government.

This is actually good news because it means there is an enormous opportunity right now to immediately differentiate yourself from your competitors simply by building a strong brand. This window of opportunity won't last long; very soon most organisations will come to focus a lot more attention on this strange, nebulous thing called branding.

In this chapter we cover the basic stuff a CEO and senior managers need to know about branding. I could write a whole book on just this stuff but others have already done it, and really, you don't need to know it all.

While some of the brand fundamentals may not be directly relevant to your organisation, you still need to know how it all fits together in order to really drive your brand.

The role of the non-profit brand

The brand is so much more than just a tool to raise your profile. There are three key functions of a non-profit brand:

1   To build awareness, trust and credibility in external audiences.

2   To build internal cohesion by creating team alignment between the individual's personal values and the organisation's values.

3   To drive fundraising, advocacy and the long-term social impacts of your Mission.

As a result, the effectiveness of the non-profit brand can be seen in:

• the commitment, pride and team alignment of your staff

• the success of your partnerships

• your ability to attract new donors, supporters and partners

• the willingness of your team to embrace change.

For more on this topic, see, 'The role of the brand in the nonprofit sector', Nathalie Kylander and Christopher Stone, *Stanford Social Innovation Review*, 2012.

Loyalty beyond reason

Brands send messages. It's been said that on any average day we may see between 5,000 and 10,000 brands. If you go to the supermarket, this figure can jump to 40,000 brands. How many do we actually remember, let alone notice? You need to somehow 'cut through the clutter'.

Add to that confusion the fact that we now live in the age of the 'experience' brand, so that means multiple messages in real time. Great brands must now offer a distinct customer 'experience'. (Why do you think so many corporate partners want team volunteering experiences for their staff? Why do you think social media goes nuts over the City2Surf and the hundreds of other public sporting and fundraising events?)

Everyone's running, cycling, walking or blogging for something these days. As I mentioned earlier, all this activity is not about money at all; it's about meaning.

We are tribal beings. We need to belong. The brands that inspire loyalty beyond reason – such as Apple, Greenpeace, Google, Nike, Cancer Council – do so because their followers believe in them, and by supporting those brands they believe they are saying something to the world about themselves.[27]

Brands that can create a unique, memorable experience will inspire loyalty beyond reason. Apple never just promotes their technology; it's always the promised 'experience' it delivers. The good news is that you don't need a lot of money to create a memorable experience for your customer – you just need to make it personal.

---

27   The phrase 'loyalty beyond reason' comes from Kevin Roberts in his seminal work on brands, *Lovemarks: the Future of Brands*, Murdoch Books, 2004.

Marketing to millennials

This whole experience thing is particularly true for the millennials (the generation born 1982 to 2004). They are very civic minded, environmentally conscious and demand social responsibility from their employers. This was the 'every kid gets a trophy' generation. For millennials, customisation is key. They search for products that make them feel unique. This is about identity. As a result, they want an interaction that goes way beyond the transaction and social media provides the fuel to fan the flame. (If you're not already a registered charity on the online fundraising platforms Everyday Hero or Go Fundraise you should definitely consider it.)

Your brand ambassadors

Great brands offer a very specific, unique kind of value and they usually drive this message home by using brand ambassadors, who put a face to the brand. Putting a human face – a human touch – to your brand experience can supercharge your marketing.

The Fred Hollows Foundation are master marketers and fundraisers in the Australian non-profit space. Back in 2011, I was privileged to hear Nicola Stewart, then Director of Fundraising, speak at a conference about how, back in 2005, the Fred Hollows Foundation was struggling with their fundraising. They knew they had to fix things, and they knew it was a branding issue.

So they went back to the brand basics, returning to the original Fred Hollows storyline, featuring Fred as the brand ambassador supported by iconic imagery, creating a clear and consistent brand with a strong call to action – *'Restore sight for $25'* – and backing it all in with powerful individual stories. They've never looked back. Today, they are still one of the most successful non-profit brands in this country.

Your logo

A strong logo is simple, memorable and timeless (think Cerebral Palsy Alliance, Amnesty International, Landcare Australia).

Finding a logo that fits your organisation can be a lengthy process. You need to know your key target markets, and then go out and test your designs and find out which ones resonate with your Mission, Vision and values. This also means finding a good graphic designer who is prepared to spend the time to understand what makes your organisation unique.

If you don't already have a strong logo then it may be simply a matter of upgrading your current logo to create something that puts more impact and relevance behind your message.

Be very careful about completely re-branding. There are many agencies that jump in and do exactly that for every new client. This risks the goodwill and loyalty (or 'brand equity') that your brand has built up over many years, internally and externally.

Your tagline

Your tagline is a positioning statement that defines and distinguishes the business. It makes it clear who you are and who you are not. It should be simple and inspiring. It should be a key part of your identity, not just your product offer.

The tagline is best written after you've clearly defined your key target markets because it needs to reflect your competitive positioning and your brand values. If you nail this, it will significantly strengthen your brand.

In July 2015, Revolutionise, a highly respected UK fundraising consultancy, released the results of their study of 300 successful non-profits. Each charity in the survey was known for its awesome fundraising and strong brand proposition. The very best had what

Alan Clayton, a Director of Revolutionise, called 'audaciously ambitious' taglines.[28]

Cancer Research UK: *Together we will beat cancer.*
Save the Children: *No child born to die.*
Cystic Fibrosis Trust: *We won't celebrate turning 50 until everyone can.*
Youth Mental Health, Norway: *Nobody should feel so bad that death is the only way out.*

Impossible taglines are magic. The promises embedded within these taglines gave donors something to believe in, creating a powerful emotional connection and a strong financial response.

I'm not saying we should make impossible promises, I'm just saying that every so often we need to be bolder and more visionary in our thinking, because everywhere, everyday people are looking for a cause to believe in; one that helps them better define themselves; one that gives their life more meaning.

Your style guide

A style guide is a set of standards for the design of your logo, artwork templates and documents. Its purpose is to protect your brand. It sets out the design guidelines required to ensure consistency and professionalism across all your communications and ensures your brand is consistently represented internally and externally by all employees, designers, advertisers and partners across all mediums.

If you don't have one, you need one. It should include specific standards for using the logo (and the logos of any sub-brands you may have), colours, fonts and brand imagery across all mediums (brochures, flyers, web, social media platforms, signage, etc.)

---

28   Alan Clayton, Revolutionise, July 2015.

Little things are big things when it comes to branding. You have to be consistent or you risk diluting your message and weakening your brand.

Your brand architecture

Brand architecture describes the relationship between your primary brand and any sub-brands.

It's quite common to see charities with a proliferation of house brands or a new logo for every service division. This weakens your overall branding. The more brands you have the harder it is to raise awareness.

You need one 'master' brand that tells your overall story. This makes it a lot easier and cheaper to build your brand awareness. If you already have a number of brands, it might be worth working with a marketing expert to conduct a brand audit and develop an overarching brand strategy. Otherwise, things can get messy – and pricey.

A strong overarching brand strategy is one that clearly defines and protects the master brand and outlines the brand architecture. All sub-brands then serve to reinforce rather than dilute the overarching brand.

So why does this matter?

1 With multiple logos you create identity confusion (i.e. who exactly is the entity behind the message?).

2 If your program or service stream has its own logo, and the customer builds allegiance to it, what happens if that particular program or service is sold off or discontinued?

3 It becomes so much harder to raise awareness.

4 Brands contain stories – your story. The story itself generates the goodwill (called 'brand equity'). What happens to that goodwill if the brand disappears due to a takeover or merger?

As I look around the disability sector today, there are many providers considering and implementing mergers and takeovers. The smartest ones respect the years of goodwill that may be associated with the brand they are taking over. They understand the value of the brand as part of the organisational asset base.

As more disability providers turn to partnerships, mergers and social enterprises, the importance of an overarching brand strategy will be critical to protect your existing goodwill and prevent damage to your messaging, fundraising and visibility.

Brand values: knowing what you stand for

A few years ago I ran a brand planning workshop for a highly respected community services organisation. Their growth target was to increase turnover by 50% within five years and clients by 40%. However, they were going through a period of intense internal and external change.

Once again (this keeps happening), nobody except the CEO could repeat the Vision Statement or the values without prompting. Once again, there was no 'buy in' or ownership from the senior leadership team.

The organisational values you see on websites and brochures can easily be just token words, or they can be brand values. Brand values are the key to inspiring loyalty beyond reason.

Brand values form the foundation of the brand. Your brand values cannot simply be words on a page or a screen. They should be the starting point for *every activity*: from how the phone is answered, to how the staff are dressed, to the first impression anyone receives when they walk through your front door, to how you treat your staff.

Every contact with every stakeholder should reflect your brand values. This is about daily impacts at a personal level, and this is what makes a brand memorable.

Years ago, there was one word that was used to reflect the brand values of Qantas. Everything the organisation did had to reflect this one brand value. From the design of the cockpit, to the look of the terminal, to the uniforms worn by the flight attendants. That brand value was: *safety*.

The key to a high-performance culture

By embedding the brand into the daily activities of the organisation you begin to generate 'money can't buy' word-of-mouth advertising as more customers, clients, families, donors, partners and supporters are touched by your brand.

The impact on staff can be transformational. There is a strange magic that happens when individuals care passionately about the brands they work for. It happens when something resonates with their own personal goals. It's one of the wonderful things about working in this sector, and I've seen it so many times in my workshops. It all has to do with the values that underpin the brand.

When your staff believe that their personal values are aligned with the values of the organisation they work for, amazing things happen. They go way above and beyond in delivering the client experience. You begin to tap into their passions and enormous reserves of energy; you're also more likely to achieve an acceptance and commitment to positive cultural change. This is not so much 'living the brand' as 'bringing the brand alive' – and your clients, donors, volunteers and new staff members will feel it on contact!

In essence, you get to the heart of transformation.

Walking the talk: Bringing the brand alive

If *justice* is a brand value ... what would this mean for the way you hire and fire?

If *social inclusion* is a brand value ... how many people with disabilities are paid staff members in your organisation?

If *compassion* is a brand value ... how do you deal with a grieving client or volunteer?

Culture beats strategy

Every strong organisational culture has clearly articulated values that form a framework for decision making and drive daily activities. In the commercial marketplace, strong internal brands create strong team alignment which creates a strong external brand which attracts and connects with potential customers, staff and partners on a daily basis.

The bottom line here is that you can have the smartest strategy in the world and not get anywhere if your branding is weak, because it's your brand that drives long-term, positive cultural change.

Having a weak brand is like driving a car with the handbrake on. You're going to damage the vehicle, you'll never get the performance you paid for and you'll be left behind.

Collapsing the silos

In larger charities there can sometimes be a real disconnect between the 'Marketing Department' and the 'Fundraising or Development Department'. This is old school 'charity marketing' and it no longer works. We need to collapse the silos.

The brand exists to improve and facilitate every relationship your organisation has with every internal and external stakeholder. If your brand doesn't facilitate and reinforce your fundraising function then it's not working.

You need one seamless communications function which is professionally brand-driven. This means consistent branding and consistent brand values impacting every contact point, regardless of whether you're talking to a donor, a corporate partner, a volunteer or a client family.

> 'A non-profit brand that brings home the bacon is one that shows donors how your values align with theirs and how they can change the world by giving through you.'
>
> *Jeff Brooks, Future Fundraising Now blog, 'When non-profit branding does the job', 14 January 2014*

Your brand stories

We humans are hardwired to sit up and listen to stories about individuals. It's in our DNA. But tell a story about the hundreds or thousands of people you've supported over the years and your listeners will tune out. Some of the most effective fundraising copywriters in Australia (and we have some incredible fundraisers in this country) prove it over and over again with every appeal letter.

A simple story, told well, can have an incredible impact. There are some essential brand stories great non-profits repeatedly tell well across all their communications. Every one of these stories reinforces their brand values.

I think there are three types of stories that you need to be able to tell with passion (if you can't then you're probably not working for the right organisation):

- the individual stories that demonstrate your social impact

- your origin or Mission story

- your thank you story.

The great news is that you don't have to reach everyone with your stories, you only have to reach your key target markets.

People connect with the narrative of the story via their preferred medium. The channel you use to reach them varies depending on who you're targeting. Each key target market will have a specific group of integrated channels through which you can reach them most effectively. Knowing which channels to use will save you a lot of time, money and frustration.

SOME CHANNEL OPTIONS

For individuals:
- your website (must be mobile responsive)
- blogs
- live webinars and hangouts
- Facebook and YouTube videos
- Twitter, Instagram and LinkedIn
- media/PR
- third-party fundraising events

For business and community partners:
- LinkedIn posts
- Twitter
- Face-to-face speaking opportunities via clubs, councils, Rotary, Lions, Probus, associations and peak bodies
- YouTube videos
- business networking events

Your individual stories

You need to tell simple, heartfelt stories that demonstrate how your organisation has transformed lives. You need a bank of individual stories and testimonials that reflect the diversity of your organisation, drawn from varying stakeholders: the people you support, their families, your staff, volunteers, your donors and partners.

By telling a range of different stories you can demonstrate your credibility to a range of different types of customers.

Anything someone else says about you is intrinsically more trusted than anything you say about yourself.

As a non-profit organisation, one of the most powerful stories you can tell is the donor's story. Typically in this type of story your donor tells the world why *your* cause is *their* cause. We've all heard these inspirational stories: cyclists who ride to eliminate cancer, families who sponsor a child, mummy bloggers who encourage hundreds of other mums to fund wells in Africa. Ordinary people doing extraordinary things. These stories are empowering. They act as the 'cheerleaders' for your cause and they open wallets.

Your Mission story

Let's be really clear: disability providers are now in a situation where they will have to sell their services and compete in the marketplace. Your clients are now your customers. From 2019 approximately 460,000 individuals will be sharing $22 billion, with an average package size ranging from approximately $34,900 up to $54,700.

There is a major philosophical shift behind the new disability marketplace. Your customers no longer have to compete with others for a limited number of free spaces within your organisation. The tables have turned. Your clients are now consumers, who can demand quality and go elsewhere if they don't receive it. They are no longer 'welfare recipients' – this is an insurance scheme. They are entitled to claim their funding.

As a result, you need to be able to tell your mission story – and tell it well. This is the story that explains why your organisation exists, and ideally it sits **within a 'positioning statement' or paragraph that encapsulates your key marketing message. This is more than just your Mission; it's what you want to be known for in the marketplace.**

The Mission story communicates who you are, your Mission (your why) or the philosophy that underpins your approach, what you do, what makes you unique, who your customer is and the problem you solve for them. You should be able to deliver it verbally (and visually) in less than *90 seconds or 150 words.*

This paragraph can be used consistently across all your marketing and fundraising materials: your brochures, your event keynote presentations, your grant applications, your website, your job advertisements, etc. By streamlining your content creation in this way you actually reduce the amount of work and create greater professionalism across your communication channels.

Developing a great Mission story is often a matter of listening to your current customers, donors, volunteers and supporters, and asking them why they buy from you, why they give to you, why they partner with you.

Great leaders know how to listen. The more listening we do, the better we communicate. The better we communicate, the more easily we handle change.

Dimensions UK, Fighting Chance Australia and The Housing Connection are professional providers with strong Mission stories. We look at these in the following pages.

Case study: Dimensions UK

Dimensions UK, one of England's largest providers with 3,500 clients, have a range of 20 different individual stories under the 'Our Stories' tab on their website. Each story serves to highlight the individual's problem and how the organisation specifically helped them. Many are simply text, some also include a photograph. But every one of them includes a link at the base of the story: Find Support Services. (See www.dimensions-uk. org/about-us/our-stories)

Tagline: There for the people we support

Mission story:

'Dimensions is a specialist provider of a wide range of services for people with learning disabilities and people who experience autism. We are a not-for-profit organisation, supporting around 3,500 people and their families throughout England and Wales.

We have been providing support packages for families for almost 40 years. We offer a range of support services to children and adults of all ages, including those with complex needs or challenging behaviour.

We enable people to be part of their community and make their own choices about their lives. We believe that not only do we change the lives of the people we support, but they also change ours.'

Their web page is headed up with their Mission story in video form. Their video spells out their brand values (respect, ambition, courage, partnership and integrity) and the voice-over powerfully and personally reinforces the key marketing message. (See www.dimensions-uk.org/about-us)

Case study: Fighting Chance Australia

Laura O'Reilly, CEO of the small Australian disability provider Fighting Chance, states that video storytelling has been their single most successful marketing strategy. Their website has a simple, compelling video which not only delivers their mission story but also delivers the youthful energy, passion and commitment of the organisation. (See fightingchance.org.au/about-us)

Tagline: Supporting people with disabilities to reach their potential

Mission story:

'Fighting Chance is a non-profit organisation which exists to enrich the lives of young adults with disability in Australia.

We believe that no Australian adult should be prevented from pursuing their ambitions and fulfilling their potential simply because they have a disability. Yet the stark reality is that 85% of young adults with profound disabilities in Australia experience life-long unemployment and have just one-tenth the opportunity for social participation outside the home compared with the "average" Australian.

Through the creation of innovative training programs and social businesses, Fighting Chance provides opportunities for meaningful social participation, employment, work experience and skill development to young people with the most significant disabilities in our community.'

Case study: The Housing Connection

The Housing Connection is a Sydney-based disability service provider that has always been highly 'person-centred' in their approach; everything begins with the individual needs of the client. Their Mission story places a strong emphasis on their philosophy.

Tagline: Individually tailored services for adults with disabilities.

Mission story:

'The Housing Connection supports adults with intellectual and other disabilities to live meaningful, inclusive and valued lives in the community as independently as possible.

Being part of a community means meeting new people, learning new things, working, volunteering, being healthy and active and travelling to new places. It connects us with the relationships and activities we need to get the best out of life.

We specialise in providing one-on-one support to adults in their home and in the community. We help our clients connect and build lasting relationships with people, places, shops and services in their local area. We believe that every individual has the right to live in the community, to participate in the life of the community and to take up roles that are valued by the community.'

Your thank you story

Nothing builds a sense of community like gratitude. The thank you story is really another form of individual story because the more specific you can make it the more powerful it will be. This is the story you use to thank your donors, volunteers, customers, partners – anyone who has taken a step towards supporting your work.

This story makes the impact of their support crystal clear. Did the cash or in-kind donation affect a single person? In what way? What obstacle did their support help to overcome? What percentage of their cash gift went to the cause? Can you include a personal quote from the recipient of the donation? Can you include an image or a video thank you? Could a board member make a personal thank you phone call to a new regular donor, major donor or a new customer, family member or carer?

Something that will be new for many disability organisations is a personal thank you to the customer for selecting your organisation for their service needs. What impact has the decision made? Could this be a hand-written note to the person and their family? Could this be an invitation to a welcome barbecue? The more personal you can make the thank you the more powerful it will be.

Your existing customers and their families should be the best advocates for your services. The more you can acknowledge and engage them, the more mutually rewarding the relationship will be.

Your profile and the NDIS

The NDIS rollout is the ideal opportunity for organisations to demonstrate their strong commitment to customer service and transparency. This is an opportunity to deliver outstanding customer service and really differentiate yourself with the clarity, frequency and professionalism of your communication skills.

This is also an ideal opportunity to demonstrate your credibility as a professional service provider to your team. You need to show all stakeholders:

- you know what's going on and you're on top of the NDIS quarterly reports

- you know and can interpret the latest results from the trial sites

- you can clearly articulate to individuals, families and staff what the changes will mean for them

- you will continue to keep them informed through specific nominated channels

- you provide suggestions as to where else they can go for information and obtain other viewpoints in order to make better informed decisions

- the things they should be thinking of and doing now in order to prepare for the changes that will affect them.

The landscape is changing weekly in this sector. And it's perfectly okay to say you don't have all the answers yet and you can get back to them. The key is: frequent open and transparent communication.

Many organisations have begun this process and have begun informing families in a variety of ways, including:

- on their website

- by family information evenings

- via interactive webinars and short videos

- via private and public Facebook groups

- via local media.

The flipside of this strategy is that you also need to give your customers places to provide feedback to you and ask questions. Again this is an opportunity to build trust. In any personal relationship the more face-to-face communication, the greater the trust.

In times of change, the organisation that communicates the most frequently and transparently will be seen as the local leader in its geographic area. I'm not a change management expert but I hope these suggestions will be helpful.

Thought leadership and you

Thought leaders are experts whose knowledge and experience are actively sought by others. As experts in their area, thought leaders can provide personal experiences, practical insights and validated approaches.

To become a successful local thought leader you also need to have something new to say that adds real value to your audience. Being open and generous with your intellectual property is a big factor in your success as a thought leader.

The NDIS presents an excellent opportunity for CEOs to demonstrate their thought leadership and use this as a tool to raise the organisation's profile. This could be as simple as developing a local speaking strategy, which is covered briefly in chapter 8.

Be realistic about what's achievable when creating a calendar of speaking opportunities. Prioritise a few events with the groups identified within your own Living Community model. Work out what aspects of the NDIS are most likely to affect them and offer to speak on the topic. By providing missing information of relevance to their needs you are demonstrating your commitment to supporting your community and raising the profile of your organisation at the same time.

Events: pros and cons

It's all very well to have an annual calendar of communications, activities and events but what really lights the fire of an organisation and gathers new supporters to your cause is a campaign. Campaigns not only raise awareness and funds, they also break down internal silos in your organisation.

Whatever your event or campaign, you need to leverage the opportunity as much as possible. This simply means you use the event to spread the word of the real social impacts you're making in your mission. The event becomes a vehicle for your stories.

If you're having a dinner, make sure the keynote speaker is someone whose life has been transformed as a result of your organisation. Never lose sight of why you're running the dinner.

Be careful when planning an event. I've seen charities of all sizes run large-scale events that actually make a loss (without revealing that to their guests, of course). If you have a large database *and* you have an experienced event manager who knows how to run an event at a profit, then by all means go ahead. But carefully consider the extent to which you will be diverting everybody's time and energy from your mission.

The smarter option might be third-party events. This is when your organisation becomes the recipient charity of somebody else's event. If you're in Sydney, this might be the Sydney Spring Cycle or the City2Surf. Every capital city has these fantastic large-scale fundraising events that could attract new runners, riders, bloggers, fans, families and friends to your organisation. There are also the smaller scale events, like a school fete or the local Bunnings sausage sizzle.

Whatever the event, never underestimate the power of a third-party event to raise your profile, find more cheerleaders for your cause and raise donations – if carefully managed.

As with every other marketing activity, make sure you measure your outcomes. Every event needs to have clear targets and every venture must be measured for return on investment.

Massively extending your reach

In July 2014, Pete Frates and Pat Quinn, both sufferers of ALS (Amyotrophic Lateral Sclerosis), challenged their friends to pour a bucket of ice over their heads. The now famous ice bucket challenge called on people to either throw a bucket of water on their heads and post a video on social media or donate to help cure ALS.

The videos went viral. In the first month there were more than 2.4 million videos posted to Facebook. Over US$100 million was raised for the US ALS Association and in Australia $3 million was raised for motor neuron disease.

In Australia, the men's health charity Movember Foundation has raised more than $580 million since 2003.

All major charities include strong online campaigns within their fundraising strategy. Everyday Hero is an online fundraising platform that enables easy peer-to-peer fundraising. It is now possible for a one-person campaign to actually raise millions. Social media tools like Facebook and Twitter enable fundraisers to expand their reach well beyond their marketing budget. There is so much information on this topic readily available; in fact, digital fundraising is one of the most exciting, creative areas of the Australian fundraising sector.

The digital opportunity

Around 2006 the world changed forever. Social media has created a world where commercial success is built on trust rather than transactions. There's no need to 'experiment' with a trial purchase from a new supplier if you can go online and find out what their current (and past) customers think of them.

You build trust by building a community (online and offline) of supporters who are prepared to tell their story about your organisation. Successful organisations constantly tell stories through video,

print media, or through integrated campaigns across multiple channels; for example, Facebook, Instagram, YouTube, websites and live
events.

I keep coming back to social media because it can add value to
every activity. However, social media is not a strategy in itself; it's a
channel. It can be a really powerful one, but sometimes it can also
dominate marketing and fundraising activities, almost to the exclu-
sion of everything else. Like any other channel, it needs to be integrated within your overall marketing objectives, otherwise things
can get really time consuming with little strategic impact.

The landscape has changed completely, even in the last 12
months. In order to be seen as a viable and effective organisation
you need to have an integrated digital presence across a number
of platforms: Facebook, Twitter, Instagram, LinkedIn, YouTube and
Google Plus as a minimum.

In Australia, Facebook is the main driver, with 13 million users
and over 1 million contact points of data on every one of those
users. Typically 65% of your customers can be on Facebook, with an
average usage of 41 minutes a day. In any marketplace, you need to
fish where the fish are.

Many disability organisations are now running Facebook ads,
Google ads, and becoming increasingly sophisticated in the use of
search engine marketing and search engine optimisation. The role of
social media is to drive visitors to your website, so the landing page
(not necessarily a homepage) can't be ignored. (Surprisingly, this is
still a common mistake.)

Social media does three things really well:

1   It gets you reach. The ice bucket challenge example showed
    everyone that once you get the message right, social can get
    you reach.

2   It drives engagement. Social delivers free word-of-mouth. The
    better the quality of your content the better your responsiveness.

3   It can integrate seamlessly to amplify your impact. The most effective direct mail wraps social media around traditional direct marketing pieces. There are so many different online/offline combinations that can be included in a well-integrated campaign.

For example:

- **Step 1:** digital email appeal e-news with YouTube clip.

- **Step 2:** direct mail letter with (or without) premium gift.

- **Step 3:** 2nd digital email appeal e-news with follow-up thank you video.

- **Step 4:** thank you letter/digital final response wrap-up.

Key questions to ask before signing off on any campaign

1   What are our goals?

2   Is this campaign likely to be the most cost-effective way to achieve those goals?

3   Who are the target markets we need to engage?

4   What do we need them to do?

5   What actions will we take to engage and motivate them?

6   What are the key messages? Is there consistent branding?

7   Is there an achievable project timeline that identifies clear task owners and due dates?

8   Is the social media presence well managed?

9   Do the task owners have the skills to deliver their task? (If not, what support do they need?)

10 How much is it all going to cost and is the budget approved? (Have you obtained three quotes from different suppliers?)

11 How will we measure the effectiveness of this strategy? (What are the KPIs we will use to measure success? For example, website visits, open and click through rates to email fundraising, number of inquiries, response rates, ROI, new supporters and volunteers, media mentions.)

A Toy Story

I spent my early career in the Australian toy industry where I managed product brands such as Cabbage Patch Kids, GI Joe and Transformers. In this industry, products live and die on the strength of their brand. Some products are launched with only a 12-week lifecycle, so we often had a very small window of opportunity to succeed or crash spectacularly. It was a great training ground.

I always knew when it was school holidays because the phones never stopped ringing. Back in those days I could passionately get behind this type of brand and sell it for all I was worth. I lived, ate, slept and breathed my brands.

When I was managing Cabbage Patch Kids I had a Kid named Lucille in the front passenger seat of my car for six months. When I managed GI Joe, I had a miniature Tiger Shark helicopter hanging from the roof of my office and an action figure pilot suspended from a parachute over my desk.

Ask yourself: Are you passionate about your brand? If not, do something about it now, or it will be a total handbrake on your organisation's growth.

Summary

▶ A strong brand will make you an immediate stand-out in today's disability sector.

▶ A strong brand will unite, promote and drive fundraising.

▶ Great brands make it personal and provide experiences.

▶ Brand ambassadors add a face to the brand.

▶ Your logo and tagline define and position the business.

▶ A style guide and clear brand architecture protect and reinforce the brand.

▶ Strong brand values get the team on board and drive transformational change.

▶ Great brand stories deliver impact.

▶ There are three types of stories you must tell with passion to your key target markets.

▶ Each target market has its own ideal group of integrated channels to reach them.

▶ A donor's story is one of the most powerful stories you can tell.

▶ Your mission story explains why your organisation exists and is the most important story of all.

▶ Nothing builds a sense of community like gratitude. The more personal the thank you the better.

▶ The NDIS presents an opportunity for your organisation to act as a thought leader in your community.

▶ Don't run a fundraising event without someone who knows how to run them at a profit.

▶ Social media can supercharge your profile but needs a clear strategic framework.

▶ If you're not passionate about your brand, do something about it.

Interview with Lorna Sullivan, Director of Disability Services, Uniting Care Queensland

Lorna Sullivan was specifically recruited to help Uniting Care Queensland handle the transition to NDIS. Prior to this role she was Executive Director of the ACT state government department, Disability ACT, where she was head-hunted from her role as Chief Executive of Imagine Better, New Zealand. Lorna coordinates the International Initiative for Disability Leadership and is in regular contact with other international thought leaders in disability.

Can you give me some background on the scope and nature of the disability services provided by Uniting Care Queensland?

We offer a very traditional range of services around supported community living and residential care, none of which can remain as they are. There are 680 people who receive our support which is predominantly located in Townsville and the south-west corner of Queensland. We operate a very traditional, post-institutional, congregate model requiring significant transformational change.

How have you gone about preparing the organisation for the NDIS?

It took me 12 months before I felt I had my head around the magnitude of what was required here. This is not about the NDIS. The NDIS is just the catalyst for creating services that actually meet the needs of people.

Over the last 18 months we have developed a new service model based on new principles, approaches and personal outcomes. I've worked with senior staff to redesign our services around the individual and implement specific personal outcome measures. In conjunction with Open Future Learning we have also developed a staff training program which overlaps face-to-face staff training with online modules. I expect it will take a full two years to retrain all staff. Our investment in training has been huge.

We've now commenced rolling out our service model across the organisation and we're in the process of gathering data around the 'Council for Quality and Leadership Personal Outcome Measures', and the impacts of the service in supporting people to attain these outcomes. In creating the model we also realised that we couldn't expect our staff to deliver on something that they'd never delivered on before without substantially investing in training, and investing in training which takes people away from traditional congregate, segregate and risk averse concepts.

We have worked now with 98 people around Personal Outcomes and there are many examples of substantial progress in people's lives and increasing consciousness of our support staff around how to support key outcomes to be attained.

We are also making a considerable investment in training our senior staff in the principles of service design through engaging in the 'Optimal Individual Service Design' program. Capacity to understand each person as an individual, with a unique service, designed around that individual, will be a key to any transformation effort, and this program is one of the only programs worldwide to deeply explore the theory, thinking and practice that are required to truly design service responses built from the person.

For example, there were two people living in a group home, each with significant intellectual disabilities. They had lived there for many years with little personal growth or change. Within 12 months the woman now has her own home and has a job working in a daycare centre. The man, who wishes to share his home, is now exploring who he might wish to live with, and whether that person be a person with or without a disability, options which would never have been considered for him before.

Can you explain how you partner with people and their families?

Our approach is, what would you like to make happen? What would make sense to you? In Townsville we provide a small community linking service for 60 people. By working in partnership with a community development agency we have substantively moved that service from one where people were essentially tourists within the community, to each of the people developing socially valued roles and increased relationships within the community. People do not attend disability-specific group activities now, and every one of them is working towards their own socially valued roles and pursuing their own interests and goals. We have used the Personal Outcome process to gain an understanding of what the person believes is being achieved in their lives and have used the information from this to support them to build more robust plans that define the aspirations that they have for their lives.

Almost half of the people we support do not have a family and come under the auspices of the public guardian. This not only leaves the person more vulnerable within the system, it often results in people being deeply isolated, lonely and vulnerable to having their life potential and opportunities foreclosed.

We are now implementing a process where each person we support is involved in the recruitment of any staff we select or hire to deliver their support. Where they do have a family we will also involve the family in that selection and recruitment.

We are working to specifically match the candidate to the individual's needs, interests and skills. We don't recruit for 'support people' in that general sense any more. What is more important is that the relationship between the staff and the person being supported is strong. We can always upskill the candidate in the transactional support needs that may be required. However, if the relationship is not strong and the person is not able to work in an honourable partnership with the person then the support role will not be effective. For example, we are supporting a woman who has expressed a deep interest in learning how to sew. So we went out to recruit a dress-maker or a person with a deeply shared interest in sewing to work in a support role with this woman. One of the criteria of appointment was that they must have their own sewing machine. Knowing the person and sharing their interests and passions is far more impor-tant than knowing about their disability and what they cannot do.

We are in the process of changing all our position descriptions away from the idea of being a disability support worker to being 'community inclusion workers'. Language is an important aspect of embedding change; we don't call the people we support clients, we simply call them by their names, or if necessary the people we support. We do not identify where they live by the street name the house is on, but as Mary's place, John and Tim's place. These things are small but important as they all change the nature of the relation-ships and the power structures that operate within services.

How important are partnerships?

Partnerships haven't existed for us in the past but we're building them now and being very careful about who we partner with. We are seeking partners that share our vision of a personally meaningful future and who will stand in solidarity with people with disabilities. We now have active partnerships with the Queensland Disability Network, The Community Resource Unit, and Inclusion Works.

As a large organisation, many of the partners we are working with are small and we need to be very careful that we don't domi-nate the partnership or be seen as a takeover threat in any way. I am very concerned that small partners may struggle to survive under the NDIS. So we're always asking the question, what does an authentic non-competitive partnership look like? How does a big organisation partner with a smaller one and not dominate?

If as a sector we lose the small providers then we run the risk of being dominated by mammoth commercial 'Woolworths and Coles' service providers. What may be keeping them out is that potential customers are entering the system one at a time, so there's no economy of scale at this stage to enable them to enter.

I do have a concern that this will be the likely scenario if state governments put their services out to tender. This will provide the opportunity for the likes of larger, corporate-style providers to enter the market and the end result will be less choice and commoditised services.

What do you think are the biggest challenges facing the sector in preparing for the NDIS?

The transformational agenda is by far the biggest challenge. We've got to reform or we go backwards. The question should not be, '*How do we survive?*', but rather, '*Should we survive?*' The NDIA has constructed a program that assumes the same service offerings and the same approach to service delivery but it can't be business as usual.

Providers are focusing around how to remain financially sustainable when really the priority has to be how do we provide people with better services, how do we meet their needs? We need to focus on the transformational agenda. At the moment we still have a post-institutional model and what we need is a lifestyle development approach and service model.

How have overseas models informed your thinking?

My thinking has been very much informed by overseas models. I coordinate the International Initiative for Disability Leadership. Our role is to promote innovative development within the disability sector by exchanging knowledge and participating with each other to bring about innovation and change. Australian services tend to be deeply conservative and risk averse. The entire disability sector is dominated by rules. We need to look at both the little pockets of goodness that do exist within the Australian context and at what other countries are doing and transform our models of support to actually meet the needs of our customers.

What would be your message to Australian disability providers?

I think the sector doesn't understand the extent of change required and how antiquated the existing Australian system really is. They are far too concerned about how to remain financially viable and not focusing on how their services can better support people.

I would like to say: this is not about you. Providers are still intensely competitive and the nature of their services is so wholly all-encompassing for the people they support. People will simply walk away if you can't individually design and deliver services that meet their needs. They don't want the institutional 'whole of life' support model. You must be prepared to innovate, be prepared to partner, and be prepared to put people with a disability first.

Why did you move from New Zealand to Australia?

I'd been with Imagine Better for a very long while and I thought it was time to provide space for new leadership. I was also looking at the remaining five years of my career and I wanted to see if it was possible to transform these very large bureaucratic systems. I felt with the NDIS there was a real chance that this might happen in Australia.

An excerpt from a 2011 Conference address by Lorna Sullivan[29]

Thinking about what is possible

'If you can only imagine better once everything is in place, e.g. the funding, the supports, the building, then you are already trapped into the solutions before you have the deep sense of what it is that you are wanting to achieve, what it is that might be possible. It is dreaming and vision building that is always at the basis of problem solving. The dreaming is the thought process that enables us to find a different way of solving the problem. Indeed the reason that we have already come so far is because there have been people, most often parents, who have refused to accept reality as it is, or as it is presented to us.'

---

29   For the full transcript visit: www.imaginebetter.co.nz/lorna_sullivan_talk_2011

Chapter 7 ▶ *Step 4*

Define your strategy: know your niche

'It is not the strongest of the species that will survive, nor the most intelligent, but the ones most adaptable to change.'

Sir Charles Darwin, On the Origin of Species

Building your brand, adopting new technology and breaking down your internal silos will all help you achieve financial sustainability. However, your ability to continually respond to – and anticipate – the needs and desires of your customer within your specific niche is the Holy Grail.

How to develop a winning strategy

A winning strategy is one that enables you to 'own' your market niche.

You can't possibly develop your strategy without considering your competitive environment. One of the most common mistakes is to try to compete with other organisations on the same terms. The goal should be to deliver uniquely superior value in the eyes of your customers; value they can't find anywhere else.

Finding your niche is about finding the unique area of service excellence that you can offer to a specific segment of the market.

Textbooks call this 'market differentiation' or 'niche marketing'. The more successfully you niche, the more profit you're likely to make in the long term.

Finding your niche begins with asking these questions:

- What are our core competencies and areas of service excellence compared to our competitors? (Put another way: What is our competitive advantage? Where are we uniquely excellent?)

- Where is the greatest need for that service? Or who has (and will have) the greatest need for that service?

- What do we need to stop doing? (Where do we distinctly lack competitive advantage and lack the resources to achieve it?)

In the words of Michael Porter, one of the great strategy gurus: *'Strategy is about making exquisitely clear choices, it is not a compromise to ensure that everyone is happy.'*[30]

A winning strategy outlines the path from where you are now to your Vision.

Jack Welch, CEO of General Electric, had a brilliant three-step approach which can apply to any organisation:

1   'Come up with a big "aha" for your business, a smart, realistic, relatively fast way to gain sustainable competitive advantage.

2   Put the right people in the right jobs to drive the big "aha" forward.

3   Relentlessly seek out the best practices to achieve your big "aha" whether inside or out, adapt them and continually improve them.'[31]

---

30   *What is Strategy?* Michael E Porter, Harvard Business School, 2012, www.youtube.com/watch?v=NY4myVa5Wkw

31   *Marketing Planning and Strategy*, Jain, Haley, Voola & Wickham, Cengage Learning Australia, 2012.

A winning marketing strategy creates a unique and valuable market niche. This means choosing activities that are distinctly different from your competitors. Perhaps the hardest decision of all is deciding what services your organisation is going to *stop* providing. Gone are the days of being all things to your clients. Now is the time to be crystal clear on 'who you are not'.

What *is* strategic marketing?

'Strategic marketing is the whole business seen
from the point of view of the customer within
your specific and *unique* market niche.'

In the current aged care and disability markets it's not enough to market homogenous services and expect the same or similar clients to purchase them. These are highly fragmented markets undergoing massive structural change. For all the reasons we have already identified, strategic marketing will be absolutely critical for success.

The Strategic Plan and the Marketing Action Plan

Typically, the marketing function is seen as just one functional component of an organisation's Strategic Plan. However, if you adopt Drucker's definition of marketing (see chapter 2), then marketing becomes so much more than an operational function; it becomes everyone's concern and it can drive the strategic direction for the entire organisation.

For clarity's sake, when I refer to marketing, I'm using the Drucker definition. When viewed in this way, marketing becomes a whole of organisation orientation, where the starting point for every decision is the customer within your specific and unique market niche.

If you're seeking to thrive in any market, then, as in the small business model, a strategic Marketing Action Plan is your key business driver because it starts with the customer. It guides the overall Strategic Plan.

As a result the Marketing Action Plan and the Strategic Plan may be radically different from anything you've implemented before. This is no time for a 'business as usual' plan because the customer is no longer government and homogenous disability services and service models will soon become a thing of the past.

Why strategic planning is tough for non-profits

In the highly competitive Australian non-profit sector, the need for a clear business strategy and a distinct service offering is more important than ever. This is particularly relevant for the aged care and disability sectors where the shift to consumer-directed funding requires a radical change in the way providers engage with their clients and the broader marketplace.

Strategic planning in the disability sector is tougher than in the rest of the non-profit sector and the commercial world for a few reasons. This could be debated at length, but for me the main ones are:

- Excessive dependence on government funding has meant that, over time, the funding body has become the customer, distorting operations and service delivery away from serving the needs of the client – and sometimes away even from the core values of the provider. It is so important for providers to realise that their funder (whether it's government, corporate or philanthropic) is not actually their customer. Their end user – whether they call them a customer or a client – is their customer. This is a fundamental shift in thinking that should be informing the strategic planning process of every disability provider right now.

- Multiple stakeholders often mean conflicting goals: the board, senior management, staff, volunteers and corporate partners often have competing aims. I've seen so many CEOs tearing their hair out as they attempt to keep everybody 'on board' the bus. People sign up to be part of a non-profit organisation for different reasons. Profit is not the guiding principle. For many it's altruistic, for some it's because the non-profit is seen as part of their 'family'. In the disability sector, many organisations were created by small groups of well-meaning, committed individuals who then joined the board to ensure that their children would be cared for as they grew to adulthood. This traditional community-based charity structure can struggle to attract and retain the calibre of leadership and decision making they really need at governance level.

- The lack of clear measurement parameters around service delivery and social impacts (efficiencies and effectiveness) causes difficulties. How do you measure your social impacts? How do you measure your efficiencies and your effectiveness? How regularly do measure them? How frequently do you refer to the strategic plan or check your business plan against it? Are your KPIs in place across your entire business plan? Is there an action plan with clear task owners and regular monitoring? How do you measure customer or client satisfaction?

Be prepared to innovate

Disability providers who define themselves by what they currently do or by what services they currently deliver could have a very tough time of it in the next few years.

This is the time to be entrepreneurial; to innovate. How you innovate should be a natural extension of your organisation's Mission.

This means being prepared to experiment outside your current services and outside those of any other disability provider. This is about your customers' needs and wants.

It's not enough to offer innovative services; you need to be prepared to innovate your entire business model.

Ask yourself: if your organisation was actively fulfilling its Mission, what new services could it provide? What type of organisational structure would best deliver that new service?

Why you need to niche

The more you can niche your service offering to meet a distinct market gap and really evolve your business model to meet a niche, the easier it will be to find customers. This is where your competitive advantage is. Most organisations fail to really identify their ideal niche. The bonus is that your marketing tactics can be far more targeted and cost effective.

Niche success

Each of the organisations below have created innovative services as well as innovative business models:

Fighting Chance: This Sydney-based disability provider provides innovative work opportunities for young people with profound disabilities. Their market is not simply business services for adults with disabilities of all ages and disabilities. Their specific focus is on innovative employment solutions and supports that provide young people with profound disabilities with meaningful work. They're 'not trying to offer everything to everyone'.

Clickability: This Melbourne-based organisation offers an innovative rating and review website for disability clients, providing transparent information in an independent online platform. Their market is not just people seeking service provider information, but specifically people looking for reliable, firsthand knowledge from clients and their families.

Gigbuddies: An initiative of ACL Disability Services in Sydney, Gigbuddies enables people with disabilities to stay out late with friends and enjoy live music. Their market is not just people who are looking for a recreational program. It's people who love hearing live music and want to share it regularly with other people who feel the same. It's implemented via an innovative, incredibly successful volunteer-based business model.

What do you need in a Marketing Action Plan?

Strategy is nothing without implementation. A strategic Marketing Action Plan is one that identifies your ideal niche, your core services, your key target markets and messages, your marketing objectives, the strategies to achieve them and the KPIs, due dates and task owners to implement them. It's a practical, working document intended for monthly or quarterly review. It's not something that sits on a shelf. In chapter 10 I will step you through the process I use to create this incredibly helpful document.

Summary

▶ Knowing and owning your ideal market niche is the key to a winning strategy.

▶ Effective marketing plans are built one step at a time with a few basic building blocks.

▶ Strategic marketing is the whole business seen from the point of view of the customer within your specific and unique market niche.

▶ Strategic planning is particularly tough in the non-profit sector.

▶ The more you niche your services and evolve your business model to meet a distinct unmet market need, the easier it will be to attract customers, partners, staff and dollars.

▶ A Marketing Action Plan should identify your key target markets, your niche and marketing messages (or 'value proposition'), your core services, your marketing objectives and strategies, KPIs, due dates and task owners.

Interview with Kerry Stubbs, CEO and Managing Director, Northcott

Northcott supports people with disability in NSW and the ACT. Kerry Stubbs has been CEO and Managing Director of Northcott for the last eight years and recently made Pro Bono Australia's Impact 25 List of the most influential people in the social services sector in this country.

In the last year, Northcott experienced 25% growth, with 800 staff providing support to more than 5,000 children and adults in over 50 locations.

Northcott have been preparing for the NDIS for the last five years. This has been a whole of organisation transformation, including new technologies and cultural change programs designed to place the customer at the centre of everything they do and make customer service the priority.

Partnerships are a key component of their long-term organisational strategy. Their marketing strategy combines a strong, grass-roots community engagement model with the deliberate pursuit of profile through innovation. Northcott were the only not-for-profit to be listed on the 2015 *BRW* Magazine's Most Innovative Companies list.

How did Northcott begin?

Northcott began in 1929 as The NSW Society for Crippled Children. It was formed by Sydney City Rotary in response to the polio epidemic during the Great Depression. Back then there was no education for children with disabilities. Its purpose was to get children with disabilities back into the community so that they could have a life. It was one of the first children's charities in Australia.

What do you think is one of the biggest challenges for organisations preparing for the NDIS?

The lack of clear thinking and planning is what will undo people more than anything else. I think one of the biggest challenges faced by organisations is to be very clear about what it is they do, how they do it and what they want to do in the future. So I think working on their purpose, their mission and their strategic advantages is the biggest challenge. And I don't think that's any different for large or small providers.

What advice would you have for providers with a turnover of $12 million or less?

My advice is to ask the right questions: What is your purpose? What are you very good at and what are you not so good at? What is in the best interests of the people you are providing services to? Have we got enough money to get us through and still invest in the future? Have we got the right systems? If we haven't, what will that mean? Can we use someone else's?

Once you can answer those questions you can then set your direction.

For example, we've just taken over a small organisation in Wagga called CASS who was running a very good quality day program. They looked at what was happening in the sector and didn't think they could survive unless they grew. Their Board didn't want to spend any more time growing the service (as they all had other full-time jobs) and they wanted to ensure their clients were well looked after.

So they went to the three big providers in the area and invited each of them to present to their Board. They decided to merge with Northcott. There were lots of other ways they could go but this worked for them and it worked for us. We took all the staff and their entitlements. So there was security for the clients, the staff, and the service was able to continue seamlessly.

As a sector I think we can be much more commercial and still be values based. I don't actually think there is a conflict. I came from St. Vincent's Hospital and the Sisters there used to say, 'There is no mission without margin,' and they've been successfully running hospitals for over 160 years!

If you're a values-based organisation and you're wasting money through inefficiencies then you're not living according to your values.

The other advice I'd give to any CEO is that you have to learn to express the changes that are necessary in the language that staff understand. So you have to continually interpret how these changes are serving the purposes of the organisation as well as the needs of your clients.

How is Northcott preparing for the NDIS?

We were actively involved in the *Every Australian Counts* campaign early on and we're now in the middle of our second three-year Strategic Plan, which focuses on preparation for the NDIS.

We've put a lot of investment into technology and we've done a lot of work in changing our work processes and practices so that as much as possible can be automated.

We were clear from the start that we had to become more customer focused, so the systems we put in place we designed to ensure that everything flows around the customer. The goal is to free up staff so they can spend more time with clients. There's also been a lot of work done to support the cultural changes needed to ensure that everyone understands why we need more efficiencies and productivity.

We've also invested money in new staff to assist us with understanding our customers and customer segmentation, market research, sales planning and lots of things that we had not previously needed to do.

Our marketing strategy is still evolving. Our real focus is on sticking to our purpose, which is all about three things: integrity, inclusion and innovation. We've put a lot of time, energy and thought into how we can become a more innovative organisation.

Last year we won the Minister's Disability Innovation Award and were the only not-for-profit on the 2015 *BRW* Most Innovative Companies list. We've also opened a new subsidiary company, Northcott Innovation. So we're positioning ourselves and transforming ourselves at the same time.

Through our innovation strategy we've established partnerships with the Commonwealth Bank and with UTS with whom we're doing a social design project at the moment on disability housing. It's a massive issue. We want to stretch our thinking and help our staff to think differently so that we all keep thinking of innovative ways to satisfy the needs of our clients.

These are not fundraising partnerships; these are partnerships to help drive our thinking further. We've also spent a lot of time talking with clients and developing client ambassadors and champions who can be part of the co-design process. They challenge us to come up with better ideas and new ways of doing things.

How are you helping clients and their families prepare for the NDIS?

The more our staff know, the better they can support our clients. We're learning all the time from being involved in the trial sites, and this sharpens the way we can answer questions. We're running family information days for clients and working closely with our clients and their families so they are well prepared before their planning meeting.

We always make it a priority to give time and energy to the NDIA. It's good manners, it's good practice and it means the best result for our clients.

We have also developed our own costing tools. We recently worked with the NDIA through the transition stage of one of our group home complexes. We've now developed our own costing tool which enables us to better support clients moving from a group home funded by ADHC to a group home funded by the NDIS.

How important are your partnerships?

Our type of organisation only exists because of community support and partnership support. We don't belong to ourselves, we belong to the community.

Northcott started because the community started us. The money came from Rotary club members who went from house to house door-knocking and collecting money from people during the Great Depression. It was community that did that. So I think partnerships are extremely important. We have partnerships with government, with corporates, with funders, volunteers, families, universities and students. The more we can reach out and keep those partnerships solid, the more we do.

How important is the Northcott brand?

The brand is very important but it doesn't have to be totally well known. We're not a mass market brand. We don't have to be well known to the whole community like a Smith Family or a Salvation Army. That's only important if you're living by fundraising. We need fundraising but that's not how we live. We only need to be very well known in our particular market. So our brand is really important for potential customers as well as those we want to partner with.

What is really important is maintaining the integrity of our brand. I'm always very concerned with two things:

- The way we treat clients: We have an automated incident management system and I see all complaints and incidents. We should never mistreat our clients and the first thing that will ruin your brand is to ruin your reputation by treating clients badly.

- The second thing that will destroy your brand is how your staff feel. They can degrade the brand more quickly than anything. There's no point telling people how great you are and then they talk to a staff member who says it's a shocking place to work. We use our values to judge things by. And we turn them into behaviour statements so we can measure the behaviours and link them back to employee performance and our awards systems.

For me the brand is really important, but it's how you protect that brand and keep its integrity that's more important. It's more important than how you get your brand 'out there'.

What's been the most successful marketing strategy you've employed?

The focus on innovation has been a very successful strategy and we've received a lot of great free publicity and recognition. Our person-centred focus has also been extremely successful. Over the last few years we've developed some clients as person-centred champions. We put them through public speaking training and they now deliver seminars to other clients and community groups and speak at conferences. We've experienced 25% growth in the last 12 months and a lot of that's been through word of mouth. Other clients recommend us.

For the last five years we've also been running our *Walk with Me* event. It's all about people with disability and people without disability walking together to celebrate inclusion. This year we opened it up to other organisations to join us. So it's both a branding strategy and a community engagement strategy.

Interview with Dr Guy Turnbull, Managing Director, Care and Share Associates (CASA) UK

The 'personalisation' of social services was introduced in the UK in 2007, creating massive change in both the aged care and disability sectors that together form the 'social care' sector.

Care and Share Associates (CASA Ltd. UK) is a social enterprise in which the workforce are the owners. CASA was established in 2004 as a growth vehicle for the successful Sunderland Home Care Associates model, firstly through a social franchise model, and now as a single employee-owned company. Their 800 staff deliver 17,500 hours of support per week across six territories. CASA is now the number one employee-owned domiciliary care company in the north of England.

As CASA's Managing Director and one of the organisation's Founders, Guy's focus is driving CASA's strategic and business development. He is responsible for development of new territories, existing territory diversification, employee engagement, new product development, strategic business and financial planning.

Can you give me a feel for the shape of the UK social care market?

The UK market is changing rapidly. We've got some huge demographic pressures as you have in Australia with an ageing population. The second challenge is an ageing workforce. The third challenge has been the UK's austerity policy, which has brought considerable downward pressure on publicly funded social care.

The policy response has been one of rationing and deregulation of the market. The third response has been a blurring between what is a local government responsibility (aged care and disability care) and what is national NHS care. So for us as a social enterprise we are now supporting much more vulnerable, disabled individuals with the same workforce. We are delivering much more complex care, home ventilation, peg feeding, end-of-life palliative care in people's homes. So the actual scope of domiciliary care has changed and that's a more efficient way of delivering care.

What place in the market are other large commercial providers holding?

The private sector delivers the vast majority of domiciliary care in the UK – over 90% is now delivered by the private and independent sector. The real push for privatisation started in 1993 with the Care and Community Act which made local authorities outsource up to 80% of their social care. The NHS, it's still very much public sector, and free at the point of delivery. However, some would argue recent changes to the organisation of the NHS amount to a 'creeping privatisation'.

How do you remain financially sustainable under the CASA model?

We converted from the social franchise system to a single employee-owned company, so the franchisor essentially has become owned by the whole workforce. The reason we did this was because of the way the procurement environment is changing in the UK. You need to be a big company in order to be able to tender for government services. We currently tender through six local authorities. Social care includes mainly domiciliary care for the aged and for adults with challenging behaviours and complex learning difficulties.

In terms of financial viability in domiciliary care, scale is important because the margins are so skinny. As a single employee-owned company we're able to achieve economies of scale with our back-room systems and finance functions, business development, etc.

What are some of the big advantages of the employee-owned model?

High-quality care and support is all about the workforce. It's all about continuity of care and incentivising quality within a model of care. If you have a stake in what you do, you share the benefits and you understand that you have to deliver a quality service.

One of the main things that is important to the people in our services is continuity of quality care. In the UK local staff turnover is a real problem. Engaged employee owners provide the highest quality care and lowest staff turnover, making the business more successful. And profits are then reinvested in staff and growth.

The way CASA provides care and support is shaped by a belief in mutuality, participation and quality, which is shared across the company's workforce. Providing high-quality care for service users is the primary concern. The employee-owned form of a social and ethical business model offers a serious alternative to the large 'for private profit' providers.

What would be your message to Australian providers based on your experience?

You need to embrace the fact that change is happening and that it will require a top-to-bottom change in how you operate your organisation. From your risk assessments, to how you recruit and manage staff, how you involve disabled people in the design of the service, there is a whole range of changes. This is very much a 'whole of business model' change. Because you're going from block grants to individual service funds, systems – for example – need to have the functionality to accommodate individual customers buying different types of services.

But more importantly at the moment the customer and the consumer are two different people. So the customer is the government and the consumer is the disabled person. The NDIS will make that person the same. How people behave changes because of that, how you market to people will change because of that. I always say that if you ask disabled people, commissioners and providers what they want they all want the same thing: security and safety, quality and value for money, and it's only a transparent design and operation that delivers that and that's what we've tried to do with CASA.

What are the key ingredients for success for small providers seeking to compete with the larger commercial players?

I think it all gets back to where your niche is. The larger commercial providers don't have agility. It's challenging because care is about volume, but you need the agility to actually come with the innovation. The NDIS is a great opportunity to create a whole new range of shared ownership options and other innovative business models.

How important do you think partnerships would be?

I'm not sure; I'm constantly required to collaborate and it's quite a tough gig to pull off. I think partnerships are a great way to share back-office stuff so you can compete at scale. Partnerships sounds great as a word but when it means the possibility of one of the partners losing their staff it becomes more real.

The whole point of our social franchising model was that it allowed us to share back-office and still be agile at a local level – this agility has continued into our new single employee-owned model. It's just whether you can retrofit that onto an existing organisation. The whole point of partnership is to find a shared resource and that means finding economies. Care is all about making sure as much as possible goes to the 'care givers' – that will mean finding efficiencies in the central core, including on occasion job losses.

What's the next step for CASA?

Well we're just in the process of raising our next tranche of venture investment and so just about to hit the gas again!

Chapter 8 ▶ *Step 5*

Develop your strategic partnerships: connect and collaborate

'You want your efforts to endure, this requires that people internalise your cause, reciprocate, and fulfil their commitments. It also helps to build an ecosystem of resellers, consultants, developers, and user groups around your cause.'

Guy Kawasaki, Former 'Chief Evangelist' of Apple

What does it mean to be entrepreneurial? Some people think it's sufficient to simply spend a lot of time networking, but it's so much more than that. It's about being open to new opportunities to solve your customers' problems and meet their needs. It's about being *first in a market niche* and finding the right partners to help you make it happen.

Being entrepreneurial is about creating *strategic partnerships*. The more entrepreneurial you are, the more likely you are to recognise the obvious and not so obvious partnership opportunities. This is about 'sharing your cause' with like-minded individuals and organisations who align with your Mission and Vision.

Under the NDIS, the degree to which you can form strategic partnerships will directly impact your long-term financial sustainability.

By 'partnerships', I mean all the different forms of relationships you may have with people outside your organisation, because when you truly 'share your cause' every relationship becomes a partnership.

Partnerships come in all shapes and sizes

Once you've done the work to clarify your Vision, Mission, values and key target markets, you're ready to clearly identify your 'ideal' future partners.

Local businesses, local clubs and community groups, other disability providers, local allied health professionals, your donors and even the families of your clients can all be included under the umbrella term of 'partnerships'. Many organisations are going to find this a challenging mind-shift, but if you want sustainability, it's an essential one.

Sometimes the very word 'partnership' can scare people away. It can be a loaded term as it can carry with it the implication of a formal, binding legal arrangement. This doesn't have to be the case. Partnerships come in all shapes and sizes. For the purposes of supporting positive change, it may be more helpful to see partnerships as simply an intention to seek out alliances and work collaboratively with like-minded organisations with the same core values, who share a similar Vision and Mission.

More big fish

If we look at all the data around industry trends, everything points to increased market concentration in the disability sector. I suspect this will happen at both ends of the market, as larger providers take over smaller ones and small to medium-size providers look to collaborate, consolidate, merge or partner.

The National Disability Services *State of the Disability Sector* reports for 2014 and 2015 contained the following:

- relationships with commercial businesses are expected to strengthen

- 84% of providers expect growing competition from new for-profit organisations

- in 2015, 12% expect to enter a merger in the next six months (up from 8% in 2014).

If the NDIA continues to set prices then the need for economies of scale will become even more critical. Even if we disregard the challenging pricing issues, in any industry with rapidly increasing levels of concentration it is a common-sense risk-mitigation strategy to proactively seek out and build mutually beneficial alliances.

A partnership pathway

One of the most common reasons partnerships don't work out is that they weren't a culture fit in the first place. This is why it's really important to be clear on your Vision, your Mission and your values before you actively begin seeking out potential partners. If there's no 'values alignment' it's never going to work out.

Over the last 20 years I've identified, initiated and developed many corporate and community partnerships for clients in the non-profit sector. I've learned about what works, what doesn't work and how to ensure a partnership fit.

If someone steps forward with a bucket of money to donate to your cause and says they only want to put your logo on their marketing materials, take a few steps back and ask yourself: is this organisation a 'brand fit'? Is our mission aligned with theirs?

If not, then back out. The last thing you want is reputational risk, so do your due diligence and learn to trust your instincts.

The steps below outline a partnership pathway. There may well be a less pedantic way to do it, but in my experience 'slow is fast' when it comes to building lasting relationships. This process enables you to identify potential partners who might be a strategic fit with your organisation:

1   Identify exactly what you're seeking in a potential partner.

2   Create a shortlist of potential 'mission fit' partners. Be lateral. They could come from anywhere; for example, corporate partners, community partners, local businesses, disability providers, major donors or allied health providers.

3   Identify the top three preferred prospects as well as those organisations where you may already have a contact or 'low hanging fruit'. Especially consider those organisations already delivering services to your clients; for example, aged care providers providing home-based support or allied health professionals such as the local podiatrist.

4   Initiate the conversation. Pick up the phone. If there are any doors that are already open to you then that's the way in. This stage is all about getting a feel for whether you could work with this organisation; essentially you're checking if there is a 'values fit'. If they pass this test, and you feel there could genuinely be mutually beneficial outcomes from a long-term relationship, only then go to the next step.

5   Start small. Try a one-off event or collaborate on a small, measurable project. Before it begins, make sure you have clear project goals, timelines and project owners on both sides of the relationship.

6   Evaluate the one-off project as thoroughly as possible.

7   If you choose to pursue an enlarged relationship then decide on what form best works for both parties. It may simply be a willingness to collaborate, or it may be a legal relationship.

Either way, it's worth considering a written 'Heads of Agreement', which will protect you both while you're working this out. This agreement establishes the mutually agreed non-negotiables, identifies the partnership goals and timeline, the partnership 'owners' and the parameters to measure performance. If you go down the path of a legal structure then make sure you really need one, and do your due diligence thoroughly. (*Please note, I'm not a lawyer or an accountant: if you're pursuing a legal agreement you should seek the appropriate legal and financial advice.*)

8   Regularly monitor, review and evaluate the relationship. Is it achieving the goals? How are the lines of communication working? Is the relationship on track? Is it still in line with your Mission? If not, communicate as early as possible. Otherwise you'll be divorcing before you know it.

The Living Community model

The Living Community model can also be of great value when developing partnerships. This is a model I developed for my smaller disability clients ($7 million revenue and under). It's built on the idea that you can create an ecosystem of supporters around your organisation who *share your cause.*

The model is also scalable. It could work on a local, state or national level depending upon your geographic footprint.

By sharing your cause at a local level, you're embedding your organisation within your local community. This approach to partnerships can diversify your funding faster than anything else. Reaching out to your local community and developing a customer service ethos within your organisation must become part of your organisational 'DNA'.

As mentioned earlier, people don't give *to your organisation*; they give *through your organisation* to your cause. Your organisation is simply the vehicle for delivering their generosity. (That's why great donor communications give the credit away generously to the donor or supporter.)

The way the model works is really simple. It's based on multiple mutually beneficial relationships. The disability provider develops a broad spectrum of partners to provide greater choice to their clients and better connections in their local community. At the same time, the organisation diversifies their own funding base and builds the overall community's capacity to support people with disabilities. The end result is that the disability organisation becomes an active and highly valued contributor within their geographic footprint.

This is the classic 'think local' territory marketing model, but with an added community capacity building component. It can deliver measurable outcomes at the individual, organisational and community level. Your customer is better connected and more visible within their local community, and the community itself is better connected, and, as a result, more resilient.

THE LIVING COMMUNITY MODEL

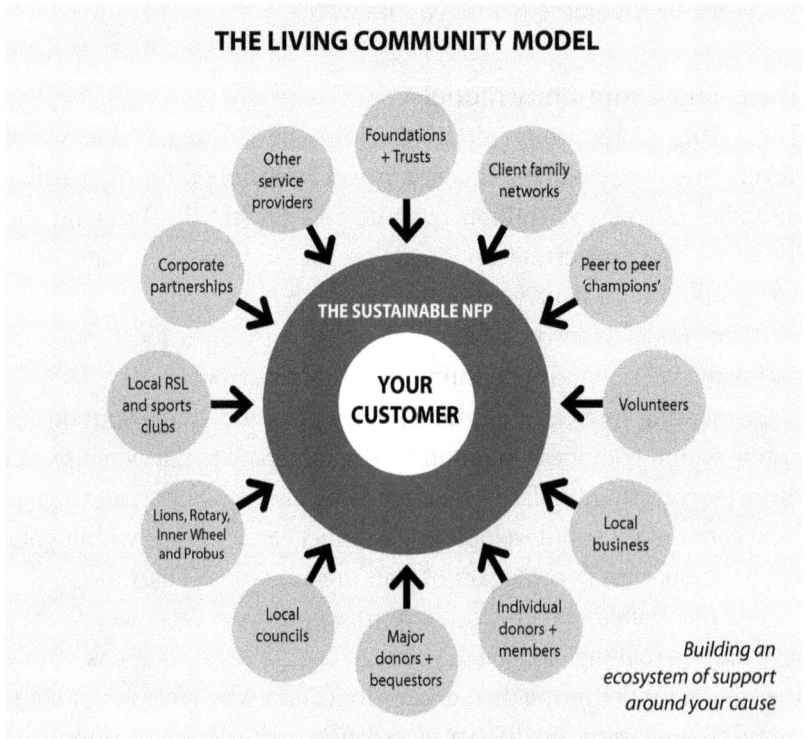

Foundations + Trusts

Other service providers

Client family networks

Corporate partnerships

THE SUSTAINABLE NFP

Peer to peer 'champions'

Local RSL and sports clubs

YOUR CUSTOMER

Volunteers

Lions, Rotary, Inner Wheel and Probus

Local business

Local councils

Major donors + bequestors

Individual donors + members

Building an ecosystem of support around your cause

What makes an effective partnership?

Effective partnerships require clear written agreements up front. They also take a lot more time and resources than you might think. So it's worth spending time identifying which partnerships are likely to deliver the long-term strategic gains before you initiate any partnership conversations. Great partnerships (the ones that yield multilayered benefits) are incredibly 'time hungry'.

You need three key ingredients:

- clear relationship owners who are accountable for the partnership goals

- a mutually agreed partnership plan with specific, measurable goals which outline the respective responsibilities (who's doing what, by when)

- an organisational culture that supports the relationship; for example, if admin doesn't talk to communications, or if fundraising doesn't talk to marketing, then you're going to struggle to achieve the level of effective relationship management you need to make this work. Your organisational silos have to collapse or this will just be pie in the sky.

Types of partnerships and making them work

For the rest of this chapter we'll look at the different types of partnerships and what makes each of them work.

The community partner

By community partnership, I mean any form of collaboration with any local non-profit or commercial provider who is a 'values fit' within your geographic footprint. Community partners can include other disability providers, schools, clubs, allied health, medical, dental professionals, etc.

Other disability providers

The NDIS is fast becoming a catalyst for a number of things, one of them being increased regional collaboration between disability providers. This is not just about collaborating to achieve scale and financial sustainability; it's about collaborating because that's what makes a community vibrant, healthy and socially resilient.

In the new NDIS landscape, other disability providers can offer one of the greatest opportunities for referral business. This is all about mutually beneficial relationships where everyone can 'win', and the end result is a better service and greater choice for the client.

For example, the NDIS does not fund training, so funding training and professional development outside your area of expertise will be financially challenging, so why not cross-refer?

If 'drop-in support' is your area of excellence, is it worth considering delivering those services on behalf of another provider who may lack the skills in this area? Similarly, they may have a distinct competitive advantage over your organisation's accommodation or day programs.

From a commercial viewpoint, other disability providers and non-profits in your region now offer a completely new B2B (business to business) opportunity for your organisation, as most will be seeking scale within their area of specialisation to drive down unit costs. It's time to search out the obvious win–wins.

Local clubs and schools

In the last few years I've witnessed firsthand the extraordinary generosity of many community organisations: Lions, Rotary, the CWA, the Inner Wheel, Probus, schools and sporting or RSL Clubs. These organisations, and many more, form the grass roots of so many suburbs around Australia.

One of the best ways to kick-start a community partnership with a local NGO is with a local community 'speaking strategy'. You probably already have something like this in place. If not, here are some basic steps:

1   Is there anyone within or connected to your organisation who would be prepared to speak at a local Lions, Rotary or school or council event? In the past I've found clients and their family members (parents, brothers, sisters, aunties) to be incredibly effective public speakers.

2   Once you've identified two or three speakers, find out what they need in terms of training, content and whatever other support they need to feel completely comfortable telling their story.

3   You don't need a fancy speaker's kit. A 30-second video made on your smartphone and a simple 'leave behind' brochure can be incredibly effective. You do need a staff member to go with your speaker and support them to tell their story. (I cover more on this in the profile chapter.)

4   A staff member can set up the speaking opportunities in advance with just a phone call to the right person.

5   After the event: within 48 hours, follow up with a personal thank you to the speaker to seek feedback. Send a personal thank you to their event host and accompany it with a return personal invitation (for example, from the CEO to visit your premises).

Many organisations don't make their touchpoints sufficiently personal. This is the basic relationship stuff that most people are 'too busy' to get right. This is about quality, not quantity; forming relationships, not ticking boxes.

The corporate partner
Finding the right corporate partner can have a significant, capacity-building impact on your organisation over the long term. Here, perhaps more than any other type of partnership, the focus is on *a*

mutually beneficial commercial relationship, one that is often extremely time hungry.

Over the years I've developed my own essential checklist for making corporate partnerships work:

1   **Know your fundamentals:** consider your Vision, Mission and brand values, and really ask yourself if this potential partner is a 'brand fit' for you and if you are for them. (Don't waste your time if there is any doubt on this point.)

2   **Be prepared to make it mutually beneficial:** What does this potential partner look for in their partnerships with non-profits? This will require time and resources on your part to make it happen. (For example, is it really worth repainting your building just to provide a team volunteering opportunity? I know one charity that did this – twice!)

3   **Be prepared to offer a multi-layered relationship:** Corporate partners only stay on board for the long term if you can build a multi-layered relationship – this means things like media and events, workplace giving, pro bono skills exchange, networking and volunteering opportunities, etc.

4   **The culture issue:** Most corporates have not worked 'inside' a non-profit. Their world is so very different, and many non-profits will struggle to meet their expectations.

5   **Frequent communication:** To keep the energy and momentum you need a communications calendar. In the last two years I increased the value of one corporate partnership from a one-off project 'sponsored' at $30,000 to a partnership cash value of $50,000 per year for three years, plus in-kind support, simply by ensuring they were made to feel like a full partner in the cause. The partnership plan included monthly teleconferences, face-to-face meetings, staff presentations, project sponsorship and events.

6   **The three-year term:** Every corporate partnership should be for a minimum three-year term. It's simply not worth the resources you will need to invest to make it work if you go for anything less.

The philanthropic partner

Over 86% of submissions to Australian trusts and foundations fail every year. Preparing a strong case for philanthropic grant funding can be an extremely time-consuming exercise.

The reason I think you need to adopt a partnership approach, rather than simply a grant writing approach, is that behind every philanthropic entity are individuals seeking to make a genuine difference. They want to be seen as capacity-building partners in your mission. The 'one-off donation and don't contact me again until next year foundation' is simply non-existent. People give to people.

It's really important that your organisation has the capacity to support this type of relationship. You not only need a strategic calendar of grant opportunities, you also need to know how to match your organisation – and your project – with the right trust and foundation, and then be able to present a concise, compelling case for support. By 'strategic' calendar I mean a calendar of grant opportunities that actually align with your Mission, your Vision and your values. This probably sounds self-evident, but I know of some organisations that chase the money first and then realise that the project actually completely diverted them from their Mission.

When it comes to grant applications, this is not a numbers game. If you treat it as such, you're wasting your own valuable time. I've met many CEOs of small non-profit organisations who spend a large chunk of their life writing grant submissions. If this is you, then please, stop writing now.[32]

---

32   For a grant readiness checklist, writing tools and other grant support information, visit www.fcmarketing.com.au/freestuff

The social enterprise partnership

Social enterprises are businesses that aim to produce a long-term, sustainable social impact. Over the past few years, social entrepreneurship has been promoted as a way to address social problems and raise revenue for great causes. There are two reasons why I've called the social enterprise model a partnership:

1 To be successful, you have to view the social enterprise as a partnership between the enterprise and its customers in delivering measurable social impacts. You are, in effect, partners in social change.

2 It can be extremely difficult to put a commercial head on non-profit shoulders. If you want to create a financially successful social enterprise you need to partner with someone with a proven commercial track record to manage the new enterprise or you need to partner with an existing commercial entity.

   It's an exciting idea, but the reality of running a financially sustainable business can be tough if you don't have the right business model, the culture, the funding or the commercial expertise to drive it.

3 From reviewing many case studies of Australian social enterprises, it appears that, as a general rule, the social enterprise will only run at a profit if you have a manager with strong commercial experience running the show, whether it's a café, an employment service, a nursery or a tech start-up.

A recent study of 91 social ventures reviewed for the Skoll Awards for Social Entrepreneurship (SASE) suggested that: 'Projects succeed when they change two features of an existing socioeconomic system: the actors involved and the enabling technologies applied.'[33]

---

33   *Harvard Business Review*, May 2015.

Here are some suggestions for making them work:

- Be strategic. Ensure you're operating in a distinct niche
  with a strong future and solving an existing problem better
  than anyone else. There is little point establishing a printing
  business if most printers are doing it tough. (Similarly, is there
  any point continuing with a nursery simply because someone
  thought it was a good idea five years ago?)

- Have the right partners. Often the ideal partner is someone
  who knows your customer intimately. Someone who knows
  from first-hand experience what service is missing in the
  market. The families of your clients have this invaluable 'lived
  experience' of the issues and challenges your customers face
  on a daily basis. Many will also have the passion, the skills
  and networks you need for a start-up. If you don't have access
  to sufficient funding, you may need an angel investor or
  crowdfunding. There are several crowdfunding platforms.

- Innovate via enabling technologies. Today every service
  business needs to also be a tech business. Think about how this
  enterprise could apply technology to transform the customer
  experience. Is there a lower cost technology that could improve
  or streamline the current prevailing norm? Sometimes the
  simpler the idea the better.

Case study: Private recruitment agency for people with a disability and Australian Defence Force veterans and families – an innovative social enterprise

'It's time people with disabilities and our Australian Defence Force veterans have some self-determination in their employment options. I'm proud of what we've achieved over the last year.'
– CEO Jessica May, Enabled Employment

Enabled Employment is a commercial 'for-profit' company that provides an online platform linking skilled people with disabilities and Australian Defence Force veterans with employers willing to embrace flexible and inclusive work. Chief Executive Officer and founder Jess May received the National Telstra Business Women's Award for the startup, the Australian Human Resources Institute Graeme Innes AM Award for Disability Employment 2015, a National Disability Award and the ACT iAward for a Startup Company in 2015, amongst other accolades. The company differs from other disability employment service providers in receiving no government funding, and acts as a self-serve one-stop-shop for people living with a disability or Australian Defence Force Veterans to browse and obtain work. The company encourages employers to use flexible work strategies such as home-based work to improve accessibility and a results-oriented work environment to ensure employers can recruit from the untapped talent of those people currently living with disability or Australian Defence Force veterans who have been unable to find work due to access or equity issues.

The business is marketed and operates like any other recruitment agency, focusing on the quality of the candidate on the company database. Enabled Employment uses all possible avenues – from social media marketing to direct approaches to employers, and media exposure through opportunities afforded by events and competitions – to market their service to employers, people with a disability and Australian Defence Force veterans injured during their service.

Every single staff member working for the company has a disability, including Jess, who was discriminated against because of her own disability:

'It's very important. We are the change that we want to see in the world, for people with a disability, and Australian Defence Force veterans.'

Enabled Employment uses new technology and cloud-based computing, and its website is innovative, fully automated and WCAG 2.0 compliant for people with a visual impairment. The site was purpose built by Jessica May and the Chief Information Officer, Chris Delforce, who won the 2014 ACT Australian Web Industry Award for Best Commercial Website for the design.

Summary

▶ 'Partnerships' can be a loaded term; the 'intention to work collaboratively' can be more useful.

▶ The disability sector is experiencing increased market concentration and this will only continue.

▶ A typical partnership pathway must begin with culture fit.

▶ Partnerships come in all shapes and sizes.

▶ The Living Community model creates an ecosystem of supporters around your organisation.

▶ An effective partnership needs clear relationship owners, goals, a mutually agreed plan and a supportive organisational culture.

▶ Disability organisations need to consider forming partnerships now.

Interview with Robin Way, CEO Community Connections

Community Connections Australia (CCA) has an entrepreneurial history. Early on the organisation decided not to go down the path of fundraising, but instead to explore small business options as a means of generating income and broadening their service offering.

Their distinct market niche is communication and their culture has always embraced innovation. In 1991, they launched the Centre for Training and Community Development (CTCD) as a joint venture with Macquarie University which became a major provider of training and consultancy services for people with disabilities. In 1992, they became one of the first organisations to provide in-home support. In 2012 they received the NSW Disability Industry Innovation award. In 2013, they launched their boldest social enterprise, Jeenee Mobile, the first not-for-profit telco in Australia.

How did Community Connections begin?

Community Connections Australia (CCA) came into existence in 1987, to move people from segregated institutional settings into their own lives and homes in the community. It was incredibly exciting for people to gain control of where they lived and with whom. Since then we've continued to support people living with disabilities to live as independently as possible, often with drop-in support and on their own. Understanding what people wanted provided us with our model of on-demand service delivery.

Can you tell me about your social enterprise?

Over the years we've started a couple of small businesses to defray the funding deficits. We ran a training division – The Centre for Training and Community Development (CTCD) – as a business that was very successful in the early years. We've also run an In-Home

Support service for people with disabilities and the general public who need that service.

About five years ago we started to review what we were doing and the issue of people moving around the community safely and securely. So we began to play with the notion of a 24-hour help centre or call centre.

We had a big 'Aha' moment when we received a letter from a doctor recommending that a patient recovering from a catastrophic car accident could re-engage with her friends and her old life using a mobile phone.

We've always been on about communication, so we asked ourselves how hard would it be to set something up? Little did we know! We went to talk to the telcos. Telstra was not interested. We talked to Optus who suggested we become a Mobile Virtual Network Operator (MVNO). We purchased air time from them and ran our own plans. That's how Jeenee Mobile began as a not-for-profit telco at the end of 2013. Mobile phones have become so ubiquitous in our community, with something like 30 million handsets currently in Australia. If people with disabilities can have access to mobile services, then they can begin to move independently around the community knowing if something goes wrong they can get immediate assistance. This means greater visibility and experiential learnings for people with disabilities who cease to be identified only because of their differences, an essential step towards breaking down the barriers around disability in our society.

What we found, and we have hundreds of stories now, is that the moment you give people the tools of communication they begin to take control. For example, at the age of 70, Adrian was able to travel by public transport for the first time in his life, from his home to Darling Harbour, and spend the day there. He knew that if anything went wrong, if people didn't understand his speech, he could hit that red button (the 24/7 call button) and the help centre could translate for him. This is profound stuff.

How does Jeenee Mobile work?

We provide affordable SIM-only mobile plans. The customer gets to keep their mobile number, there are no lock-in contracts, and we offer amazing customer service and a variety of SIM packages. (We don't do handsets.)

We also provide an accessible mobile service for people with disabilities. Our 24/7 HELP packages include a 24/7 hotline, a GPS locator and a large user-friendly interface with a big red call button. As long as people own their own phones we can put a Jeenee button on it. The 24-hour help centre is the key to it. It's having people who are skilled and trained and who can pick up the phone and answer it when someone needs help.

When someone buys a Jeenee Mobile SIM plan, some of the proceeds from their connection go towards providing a free mobile service to a person living with disability who are part of designated disability organisations.

What have been some of the challenges with Jeenee Mobile?

We had assumed that the disability sector would support us but we hit the market at a time of confusion and introspection about the significant shift in service delivery away from block funding and into individualised funding under the NDIS. So our connections have largely come from individual people who live with all sorts of disabilities and their families. Then we ran into the price wars between all the telcos that has seen MVNOs undercutting everybody else; we can't compete in that market. So we are exploring a change in our business model.

We've had no money for marketing so it's all social media. We've had to do it on the smell of an oily rag. It's a hard business and is of course a standard commercial contract, and operating in a commercial market is always hard – that's life; you've just got to keep evolving.

What impact has your brand had?

We have tried to stay close to the people and to understand what they want – not what we think they need. As part of being innovative, we've always tried to incorporate technological solutions to enhance the goals and aspirations that people living with disabilities share with the rest of society and provide greater security and choice in their lives. How to sell that to the wider public is complex and difficult without large marketing dollars. Our brand is becoming recognisable but I wouldn't say it was out there yet.

How important have partnerships been to your growth?

Partnerships have been important. There are elements in the disability sector that get it and have supported us but our largest growth is demonstrated by the ways that what we do changes people's lives in small, incremental ways. This shows us that what we are really about is getting people started and engaged with the technology that is all around us but previously denied to people living with disabilities. Our partnership with Optus has been extremely important in enabling us to find the tools we needed, our direction, and to identify what technology offers in the disability arena.

What advice would you give other providers considering setting up a social enterprise?

I think people have got to take a few risks and think outside the square. You have to be resilient, stubborn and persistent. Be prepared to keep changing your business plan/model and find people you trust to act as mentors and enablers. But you've also got to have the cash. We were undercapitalised when we went in as a start-up and we were naive as well. But we have learnt how to look at ways to market directly to the end-user. Resilience is essential. Setbacks are not necessarily failure if you keep evolving the business model and are nimble enough to be reactive to constant change.

What are your major challenges going into NDIS?

NDIS will be good for us because it will help us get the word out face to face with people who will have control over what they want their funding to do for them. The danger is that NDIS could become so bureaucratised that it ends up being another Centrelink.

I also have significant concerns about safeguards for very vulnerable people as they begin their journey into community over the next few years. Our system has assumed those pathways exist but, particularly in a changing environment, many people will be exposed to significant risks and increased vulnerabilities. Our Help button app can help (particularly people with little expressive speech) to address some of the immediate need for assistance.

What do you think is the biggest challenge for the sector in preparing for the NDIS?

Many people living with disabilities have been limited to taking services that are available rather than experimenting with what they need to have the life they want. This is a huge shift for everyone – people, their families, organisations and the community at large. The NDIS is going to be a huge system and individuals can get lost in big systems. I would hate to see all the small players and organisations disappear and services could end up being very homogenised. Individuals will need time to experiment with what they want and need. For all of us, the major challenge will be moving from a traditional service delivery model to one that provides support that people with disabilities will actually want to buy. This will require flexibility and the ability to change service models.

For more information about Jeenee Mobile visit: www.jeenee.org.au

Interview with Carol Smail, CEO, ACL Disability Services

ACL Disability Services, formerly Chatswood Sheltered Industries, was started in 1966 by a group of parents who wanted a better life for their children when nothing else was available post school.

Since that time the organisation has constantly evolved. Today it provides accommodation and independent living drop-in support. In February 2015 they launched their first social enterprise, Gig Buddies, an initiative that enables people with disabilities to stay out late at live music gigs. In just five months it already appears to be a phenomenal success. Based on a successful UK model, the enterprise addresses a distinct market need.

How did Gig Buddies begin?

About three years ago I was attending a conference in Birmingham UK where I met some people from Southdown Housing in Brighton. I went and spent some time with them over the next week, learning about another programme they ran. During this time, one of their managers, Paul Richards, the creator of Stay Up Late, told me about Gig Buddies. He had been a member of a punk band with people with disabilities, and one of the things he noticed was that friends would leave halfway through the first song because their support workers had to clock off.

He realised that here was a whole group of people missing out on a live music experience. So he pitched an idea to Brighton City Council and secured funding to establish Gig Buddies. Initially he ran the organisation from his kitchen table, and now, four years later, it's a thriving organisation.

When I returned to Australia, I wrote a submission to Sydney City Council, and a month later I was told that they would fund the pilot! The entire council had voted in favour and apparently that hardly ever happens.

We launched Gig Buddies in February 2015 at the Roundhouse. On the night there were people in the room who had never experienced live music like that before and they were standing there just transfixed. There was an enormous amount of goodwill and support.

How does Gig Buddies work?

The person with the disability and the volunteer each apply. We do a phone interview with the volunteer as well as a lengthy online application. Defining your taste in music is a big part of the registration. Half the joy of going to see a live band is being with someone who also enjoys that kind of music. So if you're into jazz or hip hop our coordinator will match you to someone with the same taste.

With the client we do a face-to-face interview. They often come with a family member or support worker. We then match the volunteer with the client by age, music interest, gender preference and geographic location. Then we do a meet and greet and see if it is going to be a fit. You find out pretty quickly if it's going to work. People just click when they start to talk about the music. It just flows.

Why do you think it's been so successful?

It's clearly meeting a real need. People asked me how we've managed to get all these volunteers. It's because we've matched shared interests around live music. It's not even about disability – it goes beyond that: it's two people going out and enjoying a shared experience. We've had tremendous support via social media and from radio station Triple J. We'd expected 25 volunteers and 20 Gig Buddies in the first year but we've already secured 235 volunteers and 95 Gig Buddies and it's only July. The really nice thing is that 95% of those volunteers have never volunteered before and have no prior personal experience of disability.

What's been the role of the brand?

The brand has been hugely important. The Gig Buddies brand inspires interest. It doesn't sound like a disability organisation, it sounds very inclusive. I think it's very important to use your brand to drive your niche. I think many organisations are held back by their brand names. I think the brand should never be underestimated.

How important have partnerships been?

Gig Buddies is all about partnerships. We've gained a new major pro bono legal partner which has been tremendous. With their help, we're now looking at how we can refine and expand our model.

There's also been a lot of interest from interstate councils like Adelaide City Council and Melbourne City Council. But we want to get the model right first.

We're also looking at partnering with other disability organisations. At the moment we're doing 'Gig Buddies in a Box' and developing a training module arm with online materials so that other organisations can replicate the model.

I meet regularly with other local disability organisations and I think out of that collaboration will probably come lots of things. Collaboration in this sector is vitally important. It's something that they did in the UK when the GFC hit and the government de-funded them overnight.

How important is focusing on a distinct market niche?

Going into the brave new world of NDIS we need to be more than just a good disability provider, we need to have something that is a point of difference. We can't be everything to everybody. One of the big mistakes disability organisations make is to only look within their own sector; it's been quite insular, but the world is not like that any more.

What have been the biggest challenges?

Probably handling the response. Having to go out and sell yourself is something that we've never had to do before. Learning how to write submissions is a whole new skill set for us and I think it's very timely.

What would be your advice to other disability providers who are thinking of doing a social enterprise?

Get out there and talk to people. Look outside the sector. That's the big lesson that I've learned. Quite often I go to things and people say to me we've never had anyone from disability before. If you only talk to people within your sector you're just hearing the same stuff.

What do you think is the major challenge for your organisation going into NDIS?

I'm not too concerned because we started our thinking a long time ago. You have to change the culture and you have to take your staff along with you. I think we are lucky because we're smaller.

Keeping the families and the Board informed has been really important. I think a major challenge is just to keep up with all the changes. You can't assume that you know something because you're told it in February because it's now July and things may have changed.

What do you think is the biggest hurdle for the sector with the NDIS?

One of the major challenges for all organisations is that the NDIS has raised family expectations and it's the organisations that will bear the criticism if they can't be met.

The other hurdle is staff. NDS has said to us that when this Scheme rolls out around Australia we will need 550,000 more staff than we already have in the sector. And that's if no staff ever leave. That's a massive number of people to on-board and upskill. How do you attract talent and how do you pay for staff training? There are so many things to be sorted.

In the UK it is the small, innovative organisations that have actually flourished since the government defunded them. When they went to individualised funding overnight some years ago many clients went to the bigger, commercial providers offering discounted services. But they soon discovered these providers couldn't offer what they were looking for.

During this time the small providers had to be really smart and learn very quickly how to hang in there, and how to innovate. It was a really lean period for the small providers who became much more efficient and innovative. I often wonder if our continued government funding has made our sector a little complacent.

Interview with Paul Richards, Director, Stay Up Late

Paul is part-time Director and co-founder of the UK charity Stay Up Late, which promotes active social lives for people with learning disabilities. He is also the Co-Production Adviser at Think Local Act Personal, a national partnership of more than 50 organisations committed to transforming health and social care. Prior to this he was the Involvement Manager at Southdown Housing Association where he developed a range of ways to enable people who use services to be meaningfully involved in the delivery of them. Paul is passionate about reducing social isolation and inequalities.

How did Stay Up Late begin and how does it work?

Our charity had its origins in the punk band Heavy Load. We formed in 1997 and all met as either service users or support staff from Southdown Housing, a not-for-profits provider of support services for people with learning disabilities and mental health issues. The idea to start the band came from Jim who loved music and playing guitar in his bedroom. One day his support worker asked him if he'd like to do anything else and he said, 'I'd like to be in a band'. We were able turn his passion into a band (we formed a week after he had the idea) and ended up regularly playing across the UK.

Unfortunately one of the common features of our gigs was that our fans would leave at 9 pm, just as we got on stage, because their support workers finished work at 10 pm. This really irritated us and started us thinking about how we could support people with learning disabilities to be able to have an active social life just like anyone else.

That's how Stay Up Late started, as a grass-roots campaign, with a simple call to action: 'We want to Stay Up Late, we want to have some fun!'

There are two main areas of our work: our campaigning side is about changing cultures and attitudes around personalisation and it has a national reach. It's more like a social movement. The other side of our work is Gig Buddies, a volunteer program which runs in the county of Sussex. This program matches people with learning disabilities with a volunteer Gig Buddy who shares the same love of music. It's created an enormous amount of interest.

How would you describe Stay Up Late?

We're an officially registered charity and we are looking at how we can use social franchising to support ourselves. We have a list of about 115 organisations who have said they are keen to be involved in replicating our model. We're currently working with ACL Disability Services in Australia and we recently met with people from Auckland, Wales and Scotland.

What's the size and reach of Stay Up Late?

We're still quite small; this year our turnover will probably be about £80,000. We employ one full-time worker and three part-time workers. We have about 60 volunteers and support 60 participants. We've restricted the program reach for two reasons: because of where the funding comes from, and because it's very important to build relationships with individuals in those areas.

How is it funded?

It's funded by local government councils and some local charitable trusts. We've also just received some huge support from the National Lottery which should enable us to operate for the next three years. We get in-kind support in the form of free band tickets and quite a number of our volunteers don't like claiming expenses. We're working with Portsmouth City Council to see if we can use people's personal budgets to fund the infrastructure of the program under some membership-based scheme. We're currently looking at ways to build a more sustainable model that is not reliant on government grants.

What have been the major challenges?

The biggest challenge has been the endless hours it's taken to get to this point to make things happen. Sometimes it feels painfully slow to get things going. We've tried to answer every email and enquiry call. It's fabulous how much interest there is.

What impacts does the Gig Buddies program deliver?

Whilst this whole program is about going out and having fun there's a lot of other really important stuff going on like developing friendships, building social support networks, improving mental health outcomes, as well as community capacity building through volunteers. One of the things we want to do with the new lottery funding is to conduct a thorough independent evaluation of the outcomes we're achieving – which will enable us to grow the business model.

What's the state of the UK social care sector?

The sector is hugely diverse with very large commercial players and lots of medium and micro-size providers, some of which are run as social enterprises, some are run as profit-making commercial providers. It creates tension because people receive funding from health, from social services and from housing. Organisations are focused on providing services rather than being focused on the perspective of the individuals who need the support.

There's this mood which feels like 'the race to the bottom' where it's all become about price. There are many organisations here that still need to radically reinvent themselves. Their focus can appear to be on protecting their business rather seeking to serve the needs of people.

What's your advice for Australian providers who might be looking for ways to survive under the NDIS?

Turn things upside down; talk to the people you're supporting and find out what it is that they really want to do with their life. Get a big piece of blank paper and start from there; involve them in the design from the very start.

Support them to make some real choice about that – not only the choices that may fit into specific service models. Enable them to be much more involved in their own support services, recruiting their staff, appraising their staff, and adopt a user-led approach.

Chapter 9 ▶ *Step 6*

Customise your systems: think outcomes not outputs

'The simple truth about the great business people I've known is that they have a genuine fascination for the truly astonishing impact little things done exactly right can have on the world.'

Michael Gerber, The E-Myth Revisited

Over the last 18 months, disability organisations around Australia have been investing in expensive new technology to improve efficiencies and drive down their administrative costs, so there is a hope of break-even given the NDIA pricing. These include new CRM systems, CMS systems, incident management systems, new billing and finance systems, HR and rostering systems, and mobile integration for frontline staff. Everywhere you look, technology is key.

However, this is the baseline survival stuff. Frankly, this chapter will probably raise more questions than it answers. I can't say which soft or hard systems will enable you to thrive under the NDIS. Every organisation faces different financial and personnel constraints.

But I can provide you with some of the questions that your systems need to address. These questions are about the 'value add' that will distinguish your organisation from your competitors.

The questions themselves will probably be much harder to answer than which rostering or billing system to invest in, because they're more concerned with outcomes than outputs.

For example:

- How do you achieve an extraordinary, memorable customer experience – with every contact?

- How do you consistently and effectively support your middle management to become more customer-focused in everything they do and say?

- How do you support a more autonomous, mobile-enabled, casualised frontline team to provide quality service and still achieve their revenue targets?

- How do you ensure your Board understands the degree of change required and has the skills and the ongoing commitment to support you in that?

Going beyond baseline survival requires a systematised 'living the brand values' ethos placed around every system or process in your organisation. This is the sort of safeguard that will help you address the above questions as your staff become your greatest, most important asset.

This is about having the right people at every level – and that's going to be tough. Staff with the skills to conduct the data analytics; staff who know how to measure quality customer service and organisational social impact; staff with the skills to provide supportive team feedback and training; and board members who are prepared to open doors. This is the human stuff which you only get with strong leadership and the right people on the team and supporting the team.

The NDIS isn't simply requiring organisations to create better marketing plans, it's requiring organisations to transform themselves.

This requires strong, visionary and visible leadership from the board, the CEO and senior management.

Change actually requires a laser focus on outcomes rather than processes. The organisations that succeed will be those with leaders who can link the changes required to their brand, their values and their mission. This requires frequent face-to-face communication at every level of the organisation.

If every member of your team feels connected through your values to your Mission you can begin to build a culture that embraces change. This gets right down to the one-on-one, granular level. This is where your systems can make all the difference. But without the personal commitment from each team member to implementing those systems, you're going to struggle.

This is a change management issue. Your team needs to understand – and believe in – the need for change and the value of their contribution to that change.

It starts at the top

I've witnessed firsthand the difference a strong board can make to the success of an organisation. The transformation from a community-based organisation into a financially sustainable, Mission-driven, customer-focused non-profit requires significant commitment and expertise at board level.

Directors have a duty of care and responsibility that goes way beyond simply attending board meetings. I've seen great charities crumble because the board has failed to step in and ask tough questions of senior management.

According to *The 2015 NFP Governance Survey* by Perpetual Foundation[34], those non-profits with a more rigorous and structured approach to board performance measurement have greater

---

34   *Pro Bono News*, 25 February 2015, 'Aus NFPs that Fail to Plan are Planning to Fail' – Report, www.probonoaustralia.com.au.

confidence in revenue increasing as a result of enterprise development and investment. The common characteristics of those organisations include a documented investment strategy, measurement of impact through revenue analysis, and a greater focus on director training. None of this will come as a surprise.

But what was really surprising was that 72% of survey respondents measured their impacts through revenue, rather than the impact of outcomes on the communities they served. This raises a really important issue for the governance of non-profit organisations: you need to be able to measure and demonstrate your social impacts and the relevance of your Mission to your potential donors, partners, supporters and philanthropists.

Qualitative and quantitative outcomes of your social impacts both need to be measured; for example, do the families of your clients feel informed and supported? Do your clients feel they are making progress towards their life goals? Are they enjoying greater personal independence?

A study of 2,700 NFP directors by the Australian Institute of Company Directors – 'The 2014 NFP Governance and Performance study' – found that only 50% of directors believed their organisation effectively measures how well it achieves its Mission or purpose.[35]

The Australian Institute of Company Directors is a great resource for governance training. With greater governance comes better decision-making, less strategic risk and a better chance at achieving financial sustainability.

Systematising business performance measures

If your organisation is heavily dependent on government then the withdrawal of block funding presents a significant insolvency risk. With 33% of disability organisations having only three months'

---

35   'NFP Governance and Performance Study 2014', Australian Institute of Company Directors, www.companydirectors.com.au

spending reserves and wafer-thin margins this risk becomes very real for many.

The intense structural change facing the disability sector has heightened the need for organisations to have more robust systems and data. Measuring financial viability regularly and with reliable indicators becomes critical. The choice of performance indicators will vary depending on the structure, purpose and services of an organisation.

Some sample performance measures are listed below. Broadly speaking, we need to begin to create better measures of social impacts (our effectiveness) and pay much closer attention to the existing measures of efficiency and what they're saying about the current business model.

Sample indicators to measure organisational efficiency:

- workforce: staff engagement survey, paid staff numbers and costs, volunteer engagement survey, volunteer numbers and hours

- financial sustainability: liquidity ratio, return on assets ratio, debt ratio, cost of fundraising ratio, diversity of revenue sources

- clients: client satisfaction survey, number of clients, hours of service delivered

- National Disability standards: external verification against standards

- database management: How many different databases are you running? How well are they integrated? Do you have a CMS as well as a CRM? (Isn't your client now the customer?)

Sample indicators to measure organisational effectiveness:

- clients: client satisfaction survey, client retention levels, client referral levels

- governance: the effectiveness of the board to achieve outcomes within the strategic plan

- financial sustainability: operating surplus, fundraising revenue growth, donor database growth, fundraising growth, philanthropic grant success ratio

- workforce: staff to client ratios, staff retention rate, performance reviews completed, staff training and professional development hours

- innovation and adaptive capacity: awards received, research conducted, innovations trialled.

Systematising marketing

The simpler your marketing systems the more effective they will be. Once you've identified your marketing objectives by target market and the key performance indicators or parameters you're planning to use to measure them, it's just a matter of adding the tasks, due dates and task owners. Performance against the plan should be reviewed monthly and performance monitored, measured and evaluated. The more transparent the parameter (or KPI) the better. (We cover this in detail in chapter 10.)

There are a number of marketing systems that will enable you to measure your activities and determine your return on investment for your marketing dollar. The more you can measure, the better you will perform. These systems include:

- Hiring an independent third party to conduct a brand health audit to review and diagnose every aspect of your brand. This outlines the brand strengths and weaknesses and the steps you need to take to ensure your brand becomes a strong foundation for all your activities.

- Investing in brand awareness measurement with a third-party research organisation. There are a number of research houses that can include your questions on an 'omnibus' survey with other clients to make this a reasonably inexpensive exercise.

- Media monitoring services can independently measure and gather all media mentions of your organisation and those of your competitors.

- Social media is a fabulously transparent and inexpensive tool for delivering metrics to gauge performance. You need a digital policy guidelines document to ensure that there are clear internal rules of engagement, a risk mitigation strategy, and monitoring of social media channels. Hootsuite is a great tool for monitoring the social media of other organisations.

- Every event or campaign should be followed within 48 hours by a team debrief, and a final report covering all quantifiable metrics. What worked? What didn't work? How do we improve the activity for next time?

Systematising fundraising

Every non-profit should be using a donor or customer relationship management system (CRM) for storing donor information. These vary in cost and structure. It may be a simple spreadsheet or a sophisticated database such as Raiser's Edge.

Strong fundraising systems flow from a strong customer service ethic. The focus is more on providing outstanding individual service than income generation. If you can do this you will immediately separate yourself from most other charities and you will have donors for the longer term. As I said before, this is not about money; this is about meaning and belonging.

Fundraising systems include:

1   A single donor database, which is critical for a strong
    fundraising function. Too often even very small non-profits are
    running multiple databases within their administration. This
    is counter-productive and a waste of precious staff time and
    financial resources.

2   A grants calendar of upcoming philanthropic, corporate and
    local community funding opportunities (see previous chapter).
    This is essential. It's also critical to ensure that any grant
    funding received is allocated to the project intended, correctly
    acquitted, and correctly accounted for within the statement of
    accounts.

3   A clear donor relationship strategy for different donor groups
    built on the end-to-end donor journey process (see below).

4   Seamless processing of receipts. Every donation should be
    receipted (with a thank you letter) within 48 hours.

5   You need to ensure your regulatory requirements are current
    and that you have an internal process to check renewal dates.
    Ensure that the required fundraising state-based licences are
    secured, deductible gift recipient status is obtained, and that
    you meet ongoing compliance requirements with the Australian
    non-profits commission.

6   Fundraising campaign evaluation. Every fundraising activity
    should be measured. Following is an example of some figures
    from an actual direct mail tax appeal campaign I conducted
    for a very small, wonderful disability provider which includes
    some typical direct mail measurement parameters.

TAX APPEAL	
Total revenue	$55,834
Total cost	$4,391
No. donors	188
Average donation	$297
Donors mailed	1912
Response rate	9.83%
ROI	12:1

Systematising the customer pathway

Every disability provider will have a range of stakeholders, from board members to customers to clients to partners to donors to volunteers. It's the unexpectedly personal experience that will either bind these stakeholders to the organisation or lose them quickly. This is why it's helpful to think in terms of pathways.

If you can begin to systematise the typical customer pathway through your organisation you can begin to add these overwhelmingly positive 'moments of truth' that lead to an unforgettable customer experience. And that is what great marketing is all about. What gets measured gets managed, so a measure of greatness is any indicator that measures these moments of truth.

In *Creating Person-Centred Organisations: Strategies and tools for managing change in health, social care and the voluntary sector,* Stephen Stirk and Helen Sanderson provide the example of a customer journey.[36] This is a roadmap that includes all the stops along the way 'where potential or actual customers wish to interface with the organisation, and a short description of how they do this.'

---

36   Stephen Stirk and Helen Sanderson, 2012, *Creating Person-Centred Organisations: Strategies and tools for managing change in health, social care and the voluntary sector,* Jessica Kingsley Publishers.

This process can be used with each key stakeholder group: new clients, families, referrers, volunteers, employees, donors, partners and board members.

It doesn't have to be complicated. I've developed customer pathways using post-it notes along a wall. I can't overestimate the importance of really unpacking every step along the pathway and thinking about how you can support your customers' experience of that step.

The end-to-end journey brainstorm

Choose the most relevant staff members to participate in the brainstorm. This will vary based on the stakeholder experience you will map:

1   Prepare a separate flipchart for each existing customer touchpoint within the organisation, from their first encounter through to the ongoing relationship or typical exit point. How are customers typically referred to you? What is a typical first contact point?

2   On each flipchart, identify all the information the customer will require in order to feel informed and supported at each step. Imagine you were the customer: what would you want to know?

3   Decide the best way to present the information the customer needs. What marketing materials do you need? Imagine you were the customer: what would be the best way for you to digest the information? Would you prefer to attend a group meeting? Would you like a personal tour? Would you like to watch a video from your home computer? Do you want a take-home information pack? Would you prefer a combination of a number of elements?

4   Identify those steps which are typically the toughest part of the customer journey. Spend some time here to discover exactly why it may be difficult. How could things

---

improve? Is it a change of staff member? Is more training required? Are better language skills required? Is external support required here?

5   Next, add in the missing touchpoints that would improve the customer experience and remove those touchpoints that are an unnecessary part of the customer experience. Are there client stories, customer stories, volunteers stories or partner stories that would help inform and support the customer journey? If so, what's the best way to tell those stories? Video? Presentation? Brochure?

6   Then add in the moments of magic, something beyond what any of your competitors do, something unexpected – something special or personally thoughtful your customers will talk about.

7   Once the first draft of the journey is completed, obtain input from a range of customers. Have you considered every sticking point? Have you considered the customer interface in a holistic way?

Systematising the magic

Very often great marketing doesn't have to cost a thing. The end-to-end journey brainstorm proves this every time I run it. How the phone is answered, how long it takes to answer the phone, the cup of tea with the family and the CEO, the personal tour, the handwritten note, and even the brainstorm that involves the client's friends and families in their own home – these simple things can all add moments of magic.

The 'moments of magic' make the interaction personal. For example, an unexpected welcome gift or kit when they first join the organisation, or an unexpected invitation to a barbecue. Whatever the gesture, it should reflect your brand values and your Mission, and it needs to be personal.

The most critical moments in any customer pathway are the first four months. The more face-to-face time, the greater the trust. You need to begin to think about a professional, personalised welcome process for each of the key stakeholder groups that interact with your organisation. How you welcome people into your organisation says a lot about the quality of your culture and the strength of your systems.

How we say hello and goodbye to anyone (staff, clients, volunteers, donors) says a lot about who we are and what we stand for. This does not have to be an expensive process, but it is a critical factor in professional customer service. People always remember what is said to them at the door of your organisation – the first time they come in and the last time they leave. You need to make it personal.

If you consider each stakeholder group as a customer of the organisation and systematise the engagement pathway then you can begin to make the experience consistent and memorable. Nothing beats word-of-mouth advertising, and it begins with creating a memorable customer experience that people will want to talk about.

Monitor, evaluate, improve, repeat

Once you've completed your end-to-end brainstorm you will have a series of checklists for every step along the pathway. You will have a new system for customer engagement. But this system requires weekly monitoring, evaluation, and ongoing improvement.

Your customer engagement system needs constant review and feedback loops. The NDIS will place pressure on all your business systems, but possibly the customer service system most of all, because this needs to be the focus of every other activity in your organisation.

As Elise Stumbles from Cerebral Palsy Alliance says in her interview:

'One of the key learnings for us is that the NDIS puts real pressure on your business systems and processes. Most of our business systems were developed with the government as the customer. That required an enormous transformation for us. Our HR, Finance, CRM and CMS systems all now need to focus on the actual client as the customer.

'That's not only an investment in technology, it's also an investment in the right people to do the data analytics. You need the right people to interpret that information to support the frontline staff who actually use those systems.'

'People will forget what you said. People will forget what you did. But, people will not forget how you made them feel.'

Maya Angelo

Summary

▶ The NDIS requires organisational transformation, not just new marketing plans.

▶ Board performance measures need to include social impacts and governance training as well as revenue.

▶ Business performance measures need to address both efficiency and effectiveness.

▶ Marketing plans must be measurable and monitored at least quarterly.

▶ Great fundraising systems flow from great customer service principles.

▶ The end-to-end pathway systematises the customer experience.

▶ Every system you now operate needs to have your customer (or client) as its focus.

Interview with Alex Fox, Chief Executive, Shared Lives Plus, UK

Shared Lives Plus is a UK network for family-based and small-scale ways of supporting adults to lead independent lives. In Shared Lives, an adult (16+) who needs support and/or accommodation becomes a regular visitor to, or moves in with, a registered Shared Lives carer. Together, they share family and community life. Originally known as NAAPS (the National Association of Adult Placement Schemes), the organisation was launched in 1992 and re-named Shared Lives Plus in 2011.

An independent report by Social Finance recently revealed that the Shared Lives scheme was the lowest cost model of support for people with learning disabilities in England, saving an average of £26,000 per person per year compared with traditional forms of institutional or residential care. In terms of delivering quality individual outcomes, it consistently outperforms all other forms of regulated home care. With adult social care budgets being reduced by £3.5bn in the last four years, local authorities have welcomed the new approach.

Alex Fox has been CEO of this innovative scheme for the last five years. Today there are 153 Shared Lives schemes supporting over 10,000 people across England, with 8,000 carers offering support on either a long- or short-term basis in their own home.

How does Shared Lives Plus work?

We're a membership body for Shared Lives carers, the individuals who provide the support. The way it works is that people from all kinds of backgrounds are recruited by their local Shared Lives scheme. They then go through a rigorous training and approval process which can last up to six months, before they're matched with an adult who needs support.

The aim is that you're treated as one of the family after you move in. They share family events, parties and holidays together; it's really an extended family arrangement.

Carers are trained and not paid by the hour. It's a unique and unusual mixture of the personal and the professional, the paid and the unpaid.

Affordable quality care in a smaller setting is an attractive and growing option for councils, health services, and most importantly adults who need support. We know Shared Lives works and offers people with learning disabilities, dementia and mental health problems a chance to stay in their local community, make friends and live well.

How do you maintain quality control?

The Scheme is regulated by the Care Quality Commission. It's the single national body for England, that inspects our hospitals and home care services. So we have the same regulatory regime as any other kind of social care.

The Care Quality Commission can turn up unannounced at any Shared Lives scheme. The inspection evidence is very strong. Shared Lives consistently comes out above all other forms of regulated care across all five of the measures.

We have a complete pack of policy procedures and learning materials to support the quality control and consistency. We also have a rigorous recruitment and matching process. The arrangement is then monitored and supported by the registered manager of the Local Shared Lives scheme who is ultimately responsible for the quality and safety.

What sort of individual outcomes are you seeing from this model?

We have just piloted and are about to launch an outcome measuring tool which Kent University developed from a national tool called ASCOT. We've also gained a huge amount of anecdotal evidence and case studies suggesting that people live quite a different life under this model than they do in a more formal service.

We recently surveyed 500 users and found that:

- nearly all had made new friends (a third had made five or more new friends)

- nearly half of them had been on holidays for the first time in their lives

- a quarter of respondents had, for the first time in their lives, joined clubs that weren't exclusively for disabled people.

People talk about a sense of belonging and ordinary family life. For people who aren't in a position to live with their own families, the only other options are to live alone, live in a group home or in the supported living model, where there really isn't any focus on the social aspect of the individual's life.

Shared Lives is a distinct choice. It may be a stepping stone towards getting their own place, or simply providing them with the choice to live with a family where the focus of the model is on helping them put down roots in the local community and make friends.

The Scheme appears to be a relatively informal family-based scheme, however in reality there's a lot of complexity behind it, ensuring that quality outcomes are delivered within an independently regulated and thriving community practice model.

Have you thought of starting in Australia?

Homeshare is stronger in Australia than it is in the UK but I believe there is no direct equivalent of Shared Lives in Australia. The Shared Lives model differs from Homeshare, in that the individual needing support moves into the household in a shared living arrangement.

Homeshare is usually an intergenerational approach to supporting older people or people with a learning disability in their own home, who require very low levels of support. The Homeshare scheme in

Australia (HANZA) has expressed an interest in hearing more about Shared Lives because there is no close equivalent in Australia.

What role have partnerships played in the growth of Shared Lives Plus?

We only work in partnership. We're a membership body so we are in partnership with 153 schemes and they have regional and national structures which we support around committees, events, conferences and with a virtual online community. A key partner for us is the regulator, and that's how we've been able to thrive under a regulatory regime. We also have a long relationship with some insurance brokers who have been able to provide our carers with a tailored public liability insurance product.

How is Shared Lives funded?

At the local level, it's funded in the same way as other social care. If you're living in a supported living arrangement, you have a social care budget to pay for the support aspect and you have your housing benefit to pay for day-to-day living and accommodation costs. It's the same for Shared Lives.

A Shared Lives carer receives payment from the scheme and they're also paid directly by the individual from their housing benefits. Nationally we get funding from government, charitable trusts and membership.

Shared Lives is cheaper than other forms of care and that's the reason we're expanding so rapidly. It's considerably lower cost for somebody to live in a Shared Lives scheme than it is to live in a care home or a supported living scheme.

What role has your brand played in your marketing?

We changed our name from Adult Placements a year after I joined, and became Shared Lives Plus, and that change has worked really well for us.

For us we're not just lobbying for a particular model, we want to be a movement for shared living approaches. We believe that shared living has a really important part to play in how we support people in life more generally. So it's important to us that our brand identity is about shared living.

We just changed our strapline to: The UK network for Shared Lives and Homeshare. That idea of reciprocity in shared living is really important to what we do.

Part of the safeguarding is to build communities where people with disabilities are more visible. The worst abuse scandals in the UK have occurred in highly regulated environments, where the only people in daily contact with disabled people are those who are paid to be with them. It is fundamental for any kind of personal and social wellbeing that people are able to live in a community where they have friends.

Would you have any message for Australian disability providers providing the traditional model of care?

I've been really impressed by what I've heard about the NDIS; it feels to me as if it's captured in its intention and structure the heart of what we call personalisation. It may also avoid some of the pitfalls.

Our experience has been that just talking about person-centredness doesn't result in radical change. The only way to ensure that people really are a part of the process is to shift power to them in a much more radical way.

Despite the imperfections in it, the personal budgets and direct payments can make a profound difference to people's lives. But it's not sufficient for a good life.

You also need to help them come together in small groups to find others who share the same goals and wishes. You need to help create a structure of supports with a relentless focus on individual relationships, community living and what individuals can bring to their community.

If we continue to see people as 'a group of needs to be met' then they will never lead a rich and fulfilled life as valued citizens. We need instead to focus on people's gifts, skills and assets.

Our sister organisation, Community Catalysts, is a social enterprise (not a charity) that helps community enterprises set up and survive. Community enterprises construct something very small and personal around the lives of individuals, connecting the individual with their community in a meaningful way. The individual enterprises don't necessarily want to grow but they could be much more widespread. I think that small scale is where the most profound changes will be coming from in the future.

Create your Action Plan

'Action expresses priorities.'

Mahatma Gandhi

So where are we now?

A strong, strategic Marketing Action Plan connects every piece of the strategy together. This means that from a single tactic you can achieve multiple outcomes, simplifying and leveraging your activities.

By now you know that great marketing doesn't have to cost a lot of money. You just have to deliver the right message to the right stakeholders consistently and professionally with every contact they have with your organisation.

As I said back in chapter 2, most people define marketing by the day-to-day tactics such as social media, PR, advertising and direct mail. All these tactics will serve to raise your profile, but they're just the tip of the iceberg. In order for them to be effective, you need to have in place the foundational, strategic stuff around the customer experience that we've covered in the earlier chapters.

You need to know:

- your market

- your Vision and your Mission

- your brand: who you are and what you stand for

- your strategy: your area of competitive advantage, your ideal market niche and the customer with the greatest need for that service

- your partners: the individuals, the community organisations and the business partners who share your brand values, and champion your cause

- your systems: your ability to deliver on your brand promise – your ability to partner consistently and effectively with every other entity in the community living model depends on this.

Building your Marketing Action Plan

Every strategic plan needs an Action Plan to make it happen. The simpler and more transparent this document the better.

In this section I'm going to take you through the basic building blocks I usually cover in my strategy workshops. The end result is a strategic 12-month Marketing Action Plan that outlines the marketing objectives and strategies for each key target market. It then identifies the task owners, the KPIs and their due dates.

It's hardly the textbook version of a Marketing Plan. Rather, it's a practical working document which is intended to be reviewed and monitored on a monthly or quarterly basis.

It takes basic marketing principles and applies them to the real-world experience of the non-profit organisation. This process works for me, however please feel free go ahead and modify it to suit your needs.

As you will see from the diagram on the following page, the central idea is that you start with your market research and the plan flows from there. The more time spent getting clear on the top half of the diagram, 'The Fundamentals', the simpler and more cost effective the Action Plan.

THE MARKETING ACTION PLAN PROCESS

The fundamentals

Market research

⬇

**Vision
&
Mission**

⬇

The brand

⬇

The Action Plan

**Key target markets
Core services
Key messages**

⬇

Key marketing objectives

⬇ ⬇ ⬇ ⬇

Target market objective	Target market objective	Target market objective	Target market objective
Strategy	Strategy	Strategy	Strategy
Strategy	Strategy	Strategy	Strategy
Strategy	Strategy	Strategy	Strategy
Strategy	Strategy	Strategy	Strategy

Why this process works

The key lies in really understanding how each target market has different problems and needs. The process creates a 'target market' for every key stakeholder group you face. Taking this approach, the needs of the target market (e.g. the customer, the referral partner, or the future staff member) will always come first. Everything else comes later.

In a well-developed Marketing Action Plan, the strategies will effectively overlap between objectives, delivering multiple outcomes from a single activity. The aim is to maximise the outcomes that each single strategy delivers to the business as a whole. This makes the Plan more efficient, the messages more consistent and the activities more integrated.

a) Identify your key target markets

As a marketer, I naturally see everything in terms of target markets. Every target market has a different composition and responds differently to different messages. Once you've done the market research we discussed in chapter 4, the best way to identify your organisation's key target markets is to get the brightest people in the room. They may be staff members, board members, clients, volunteers or otherwise.

This is not about hierarchy; it's about quality outcomes. You need to choose the participants based on who best understands your brand and the overall market you face – people with firsthand knowledge, strong personal experience, a deep understanding of your client and, where possible, the delivery of your key services at the coalface. Every person in the workshop team needs to share your organisation's brand values and a genuine commitment to the future best interests of the clients you serve.

I then use the process below:

i) Look at your geographic footprint. Take a single flipchart page and brainstorm *all* the possible market segments you face within your region. Once your page is full, identify the top four or five groups on that page that will be *absolutely critical* to your 12-month business plan and your long-term financial sustainability.

For simplicity's sake (and because it works) I suggest your top target markets could be:

- current staff

- current customers and their families

- future staff

- future customers and families

- current and future partners (you could include referral networks and donors here).

This is a simplistic approach so you may feel you need to add other key target markets. From experience, this can complicate your plan without necessarily yielding improved outcomes. Your plan has to be achievable so it needs to be able to be leveraged.

This just means achieving outcomes in more than one target market from a single strategy or tactic. For example, it's actually a helpful shift in mindset to see your donors as partners. It moves the relationship from transactional to multi-dimensional. Other examples are:

- key local cultural influencers (e.g. place in both referral networks and future partners)

- key local businesses (place in the referral network market and future partners)

- future Board members (What skills are you missing? They most likely already belong to one or more of the above markets).

ii) Once you've identified your top four or five target markets, the next step is to drill down within those markets to identify which customers, donors and partners are most likely to appreciate your area of service excellence. Textbooks call this 'market segmentation'. Within each market segment you need to understand as much as possible the demographics: age, gender, income, level of education, location, family status, ethnicity, occupation.

iii) Next we drill down into each of those segments, one flip-chart page at a time, to answer the following questions:

- What are their needs, desires, goals, fears, doubts, worries?

- Where do they eat? What music do they listen to?

- How do they receive their daily news? (TV, radio, online, social media)

- What is their preferred social media platform?

- What problems do they face on a daily basis? (What's the problem really? Put yourself in their shoes – what's really bothering them? What's frustrating them the most?)

Identify the problems they may have that *your organisation* can solve better than anyone else.

This may sound overly pedantic, however it's only when you can really answer these questions about each of your target markets that you can really begin to understand them.

Once you begin to understand them you can begin to develop a marketing message they will hear.

This is not an exercise to be rushed. Your answers may not always be correct, but at least you've begun to ask the right questions, and – believe it or not – if you spend enough time asking the right questions you *will* discover some key truths that nobody else has realised.

If you do this for each of your target groups then you will begin to see some common characteristics that will inform your strategy. Once the flipcharts are completed you should have a succinct overview and a deeper understanding of each of your target markets.

b) Identify your core services – stake your niche
Under the NDIS, your organisation will no longer be in the business of delivering services, it will be in the business of delivering life outcomes. This is a fundamental shift in the way you need to think about service delivery.

With the same group of brightest minds in the room, I suggest you take a good hard look at your current services and programs and decide: Where is your organisation *uniquely* excellent?

Is it in 24-hour drop-in service, integrated housing, youth employment, personal assistant services or NDIA plan support? The key issue to uncover is where you are uniquely excellent in comparison to all other providers in your geographic footprint.

c) Identify your key marketing messages
Once you've identified your key target markets and your core services, then you can develop your tagline. Typically, this is best done through the same workshop brainstorming process as before. Just ensure your workshop team comprises those people who best know and understand your target markets – preferably including actual representatives of those markets.

Often in the commercial world there's only one marketing message and it's used as the tagline. For Apple it's *Think Different*. For Red Bull it's *Gives you Wings*.

What do you want people to think when they see *your* brand? What's *your* promise to the market? Developing your tagline needs creative input.

Key messages

In addition to the tagline, you need to develop other supporting messages to include in your communications (online, offline and face to face). Each one of your key target markets has a key problem or issue. If your message is consistently framed to address that problem or issue then it will be heard. When we identified your target markets earlier in this chapter, you also considered their key problems. The closer you can get to understanding what's really frustrating your customer the better.

For example:

Target market: Your current customers and their families.

The problem: Many clients and their families right now are afraid that under the NDIS they will actually lose something – they may be somehow worse off.

The key message: We understand the changes ahead and will work with you every step of the way to ensure you are kept informed and supported around the NDIS changes and what it will mean for you and your family.

Marketing textbooks call this key message the 'Value Proposition'. This exercise should be repeated for each target market, whether it's your future customers, your current staff, your future staff, your referral partners, your donors, etc.

d) Determine your marketing objectives

Now it's a simple matter of setting a clear 12-month objective for each target market.

Put simply, an organisation's strategy should:

* align around the greatest potential opportunities for long-term profitable growth

* be Specific, Measurable, Attainable, Realistic, Timely (SMART).

The box below provides some examples of how to frame your marketing objectives. There is one objective for each target market and each one includes clear measurement parameters.

Sample marketing objectives:

1. **The current customer marketing objective:** 75 clients and their families feel informed and empowered around the NDIS changes and what they will mean for them. (KPI: 98% satisfaction, survey to be conducted by 31 May 2016.)

2. **The future customer marketing objective:** By June 2016, we will have had 3 separate face-to-face opportunities (within a group or individually) with 10 potential clients and their families.

3. **The key referrer marketing objective:** By June 2016, we will have had four face-to-face opportunities with NDIA planners in our region and six with current or potential local referral sources. The number of new client enquiries via these channels has increased by 30%.

4. **The staff marketing objective:** All staff feel aligned and connected with the organisation's vision and purpose. They understand the NDIS changes and what they will mean for them, and how to explain those changes. All staff undergo customer service training. (KPIs: 98% staff satisfaction rates, 100% staff retention rate, 80% reduction in sick leave.)

e) Determine your marketing strategies

In this final step in building your Marketing Action Plan you develop specific marketing strategies to deliver your marketing objective in each target market. As mentioned earlier, in a well-developed marketing plan, strategies will overlap between objectives, delivering multiple outcomes from the one activity.

The aim is to maximise the outcomes each single strategy delivers to the business as a whole. Again, this is a simple brainstorming process with your workshop team.

Once you've completed the strategies within each objective the plan can be costed and budgeted. Each specific strategy is allocated a task owner and a due date (see opposite for an example). Every Action Plan should be reviewed and monitored quarterly. It is a living working document, not a plan that sits on the shelf.

On the next page is a sample from my Marketing Action Plan template for the current customer target market. You should only need one page per target market.

The Current Customer Target Market

Marketing objective:

The current customer marketing objective: 75 clients and their families feel informed and empowered around the NDIS changes and what they will mean for them. (KPI: 98% satisfaction survey to be conducted by 31 May 2016.)

Sample strategies for Current Customer Marketing Objective

SAMPLE STRATEGIES	DUE DATE	OWNER
Schedule CEO touchpoints (every family, 3 ways, every ¼)	15.2.16	CEO
Schedule regular individual client/family meetings	1.2.16	Client Services Manager
Run 4 NDIS info sessions (e.g. public webinar or informal evenings)	30.6.16	As above
Schedule meetings with key influencers in your local community	15.2.16	CEOs PA
Distribute links to My Choice, Access Checker, etc. and establish online family portal for regular NDIS updates	15.2.16	Marketing Manager
Create New Family Info Pack including new client manual, FAQs, client case studies and how to prepare your NDIS plan information	15.2.16	As above

Chapter 11 ▶

Where do we go now?

'Change will not come if we wait for some other person or some other time. We are the ones we've been waiting for. We are the change that we seek.'

Barack Obama

Thank you for taking the time to read this book. I hope that you found what you were looking for when you purchased it.

It's my belief that the NDIS presents enormous opportunity for people with disabilities *and* for disability service providers. Unfortunately, the lightning speed with which it's being rolled out is risking the future of a healthy and diverse disability sector. For individuals and families with disabilities to have a real choice in this market we need small providers providing high-quality, innovative supports to thrive alongside the larger players.

There is a wealth of knowledge, skill, talent and experience in the Australian disability sector. Writing this book and interviewing the many generous leaders and change-makers has been a very enriching and humbling process.

Finally, I urge you to do three things:

- Make it okay for your staff to experiment and fail, and support them to recover fast.

- Listen one on one to your clients and their families and provide a range of channels and forums for sharing experiences, stories and learnings.

- Reach out to other providers, local community influencers, businesses, allied health providers, associations, clubs and groups like you've never done before. There will be opportunities everywhere once you remove the 'lens' of disability.

For support, email fran@fcmarketing.com.au. I'd love to hear how you're going!

ACKNOWLEDGEMENTS

This book would not have been possible without the CEOs and thought leaders who gave so generously of their time, support and insights during our interviews: Rob White and Elise Stumbles from Cerebral Palsy Alliance, Laura O'Reilly from Fighting Chance, Gordon Duff from National Disability Services, Kerry Stubbs from Northcott, Libby Ellis from In Charge, Lorna Sullivan from Uniting Care Queensland, Jessica May from Enabled Employment, Robin Way from Jeenee Mobile, Aviva Beecher Kelk from Clickability, Carol Smail from Gig Buddies, Steve Scown from Dimensions UK, Alex Fox from Shared Lives, Paul Richards from Stay up Late, Dr. Guy Turnbull from CASA UK and Janet H. who trusted me with her family's story.

I've learnt many things writing this book, one of them being that, for a new author, a book is a team effort. My sincere thanks goes to everyone behind the scenes who supported me in so many ways: Andrew Griffiths and Michael Hanrahan who guided me through the process, Leanne Fretten from Sylvanvale, Doug Talbert and Nicola Hayhoe from The Housing Connection, Philip Petrie from Allevia, Roger West from Westwood Spice, Nicola Stewart from The Fred Hollows Foundation, Alan Clayton from Revolutionise UK, Sunjoo Kim, Craig Hooper, Lee Gabbett, Neil Campbell, Andrew Akratos, Janet Smith, Rosemary Shapiro-Liu, Catherine Mahony, Madeleine Donkin, Joanna Lockwood from Cerebral Palsy Alliance, Tania Machon from Dimensions UK, Winnie Cheng from Westfield, Kiralie Allan, Joanna Sharma, Kerry McNally, Emma McDonald from *Third Sector* magazine, Tina Vuong from Connecting Up.

Finally, huge thanks and hugs to my family and friends who put up with me as I went into hibernation for five months to write this book.

fcmarketing.com.au

*We help nonprofits build their
brands and diversify their income.*

Please connect with Fran Connelley on LinkedIn.